SAFEGUARDING
CIVIL LIBERTY TODAY

SAFEGUARDING CIVIL LIBERTY TODAY

THE EDWARD L. BERNAYS LECTURES OF 1944
GIVEN AT CORNELL UNIVERSITY BY

CARL L. BECKER
MAX LERNER
JAMES LAWRENCE FLY
ROBERT E. CUSHMAN
FRANCIS BIDDLE
AND AN ADDRESS BY
EDMUND EZRA DAY

NEW YORK
PETER SMITH

☆ ☆ ☆ ☆ 1949 ☆ ☆ ☆ ☆

PREFACE

To MANY AMERICANS our civil liberties—the basic freedoms protected by the bills of rights in our federal and state constitutions—seem remote from the day-by-day concerns of respectable and law-abiding people. They seem designed, rather, to protect the interests of persons, frequently objectionable persons, whose claims to be the victims of governmental oppression often appear specious to men of substance. Again, the appeal to the constitutional guarantees sometimes seems to come most often from crusading organizations that devote their energies to aiding and defending troublesome citizens.

This way of thinking about civil liberties is unfortunate. The freedoms protected by our bills of rights are in truth much more than safeguards for the marginal and eccentric part of our citizenship. Their application to any form of criminal process is a small part of their total significance. They protect in fact essential social processes that make constitutional government possible, and a vigorous democracy will become unworkable when or if our people fail sedulously to uphold their

constitutional rights. Moreover, the alterations wrought
in a rapidly developing industrial society give these liberties constantly changing forms, which in turn demand
changing means for their adequate protection. The
radio, to mention only one example, creates a new di-
mension of free speech. If civil liberty is to survive in
America, it is essential that American public opinion
should see, as the founders of our government saw, that
the freedoms protected by our bills of rights are fundamental to our political system and need also to be the
object of intelligent and vigilant public concern.

The Edward L. Bernays Lectures on Civil Liberty
for 1944, printed in this volume, are an expression of
this conviction. They were made possible by a gift to
Cornell University from Mr. Edward L. Bernays of
New York, an alumnus of the Class of 1912. They represent the donor's belief, which is shared by the University, that the civil liberties are vitally important to the
social and political life of America and that the need is
imperative for a more general, a more intelligent, and
a more timely understanding of them.

Accordingly, in planning these lectures, the University undertook to secure men qualified to speak with
authority on some phase of civil liberty either by reason
of their scholarly competence or by reason of their official responsibility for giving effect to the constitutional
guarantees. Professor Becker and Professor Cushman
have made the field of civil liberty the subject of special
study for many years. This is true also of Mr. Lerner;
and in addition he has recently become an editorial
writer on a newspaper which gives closer attention to

the problems of civil liberty than any other American newspaper. The University was especially gratified to be able to include in the list of lecturers the Attorney General of the United States and the then Chairman of the Federal Communications Commission, who discussed problems of civil liberty that had emerged within the range of their official duties.

A few weeks after the Bernays Lectures on Civil Liberty were given, the President of the University addressed a graduating class at Cornell on the subject, "Freedom to Learn." In this address President Day discussed some of the attacks which are made from time to time on freedom of thought and freedom of teaching on a university campus, and stated with clarity and courage the principles to which any university worthy of the name is bound to adhere. Those who had had the Bernays Lectures in charge urged him to permit the inclusion of his address in this volume.

It was not the purpose of Mr. Bernays, of Cornell University, or of any of the lecturers to deal with civil liberties from the point of view of any partisan interest or of any economic class. Civil liberties are the common heritage of the American people. These lectures were planned and delivered in the hope that this common interest might be better understood and that the will to preserve our heritage might be strengthened.

George H. Sabine

February 22, 1945

CONTENTS

CONTENTS

POLITICAL FREEDOM: AMERICAN STYLE

BY CARL L. BECKER

Professor of History, Emeritus, and
University Historian, Cornell University

Liberty is the power of everyone to
do whatever does not injure others.–
DECLARATION OF THE RIGHTS OF MAN.

I︎N THE DISCUSSION of poli-
tics few words are more important and none is less capable of precise definition than the magic word "liberty."
By going round the world Wendell Willkie learned that
all men, brown and yellow as well as white, love liberty.
What he apparently did not learn, or not sufficiently, is
that liberty may mean different things to different people. All men love food, no doubt; but it would be a mistake to suppose that you could for that reason feed all
men spinach and make them like it. Many might be
even so misguided as to prefer broccoli. As one man's
food is another man's poison, so one man's liberty may
be another man's bondage. The essential liberties are
those which men regard as such, and these vary a good
deal from time to time and from nation to nation.

The people of the United States, for example, are apt
to think that the Russians are deprived of the essential
liberties, but the Russians appear to think that they are
freer than we are. Not long ago a Russian scholar told
me that the liberties we prize so highly seem to the Rus-

sians too negative to be of much use. "Your liberties," he said, "are mostly freedoms *from* something, whereas the Russian liberties are freedoms *to do* something." The distinction seemed to me a superficial one, since any liberty *from* something implies the freedom *to do* what otherwise the doer might be prevented from doing, and any liberty *to do* something implies a freedom *from* whatever might otherwise interfere with that doing. What my Russian acquaintance meant, I suppose, was that our much-prized civil liberties are directed against governmental interference with the free activities of the citizen; so that the American government guarantees the liberty of the individual in no small measure by letting him alone, whereas the Russian government guarantees the liberty of the individual, not by letting him alone, but by seeing to it that he has a job, a place to live, an education, medical service, and other desired things. The difference my Russian acquaintance finally expressed by saying: "We Russians look upon the government as our friend, whereas you Americans seem to regard the government as your enemy."

This is putting it too strongly, no doubt, but there is some truth in it—enough at all events to bring us within sight of the characteristic attitude of the people of the United States towards the function of the government and the liberties of the individual. We do not regard the government as our enemy exactly, but neither do we regard it with awe and reverence as a disembodied authority emanating from some mystical entity called the "state." For us state and government are one thing

—a body of men whom we have delegated to do certain necessary and prosaic things. We choose them—and hope for the best. But we feel pretty sure that the best will not be forthcoming unless we keep our eye on them. On the whole, we agree with Thomas Paine that government is a necessary evil, and that if the liberties of the citizen are to be secure, men elected to office must be watched. It is our settled habit, therefore, to view with alarm any new or unusual activity on the part of the government, and to point with pride to the new and unusual things the people have always done and will always do on their own initiative, provided the government refrains from undue meddling and minds its own business.

The explanation of this conception of the function of government and the liberty of the individual is to be found, first, in the peculiar circumstances of American history, which have made it possible, at least until recently, for the people to get on very well with a minimum of governmental assistance or regulation; and, second, in the traditional political philosophy which, as formulated in the eighteenth century, was based on the assumption that the best form of government is the one that governs least. Let us take these two points in the order of their importance.

John Winthrop tells us that the founders of Massachusetts Bay came from England to America for two reasons—because America offered them free land, and because in America they could "establish a due form of government, both civil and ecclesiastical." Why, he asked, should people remain in England "striving for places of habitation . . . and suffer a whole continent as fruitful and convenient for the use of man to lie waste without any improvement"? The main point is that having come to America people did not need to stand striving for places of habitation, and Massachusetts Bay Colony was scarcely established before people began to leave it for the same reasons that impelled Winthrop and his associates to leave England. As early as 1633 the people of Newtown, as we are told, began to have a "hankering" for the Connecticut Valley; and the following year Thomas Hooker and others asked permission for the people of the town to leave, alleging three reasons—"want of accommodation for their cattle, the fruitfulness and commodiousness of Connecticut, and *the strong bent of their spirits* to remove thither." The migration of the people of Newtown may be taken as the prototype of all subsequent treks across the continent. Whenever the people in any community were dissatisfied, either for want of accommodation for their cattle or for some other reason, there was little to restrain "the strong bent of their spirits to remove" to some more fruitful and commodious region.

And so for more than two centuries the people were always on the move—into western New York and Pennsylvania, into the uplands of the South, into the fertile prairie and woodlands of the Mississippi Valley, across the Rockies to the Pacific coast. The difficulties encountered in this search for better fortunes were many, and life on the edge of the frontier was often hazardous and always bleak and primitive. But each successive frontier was, for those who occupied it, a new "new

world" which offered to its first settlers essentially the
same advantages that New England and Virginia offered to its first settlers from England. It offered them
freedom—free land, so that they need not stand striving
for places of habitation; freedom from the social restraints of more settled communities; and freedom
within broad limits to establish a form of government
that seemed to them suited to their needs.

It was from this experience chiefly that the people of
the United States derived their settled convictions
about the function of government and the liberties of
the individual. Since there was always more land than
people to cultivate it, it was always relatively easy for
the common man to make his own way and pay his own
score. Since the people were always on the move from
the more settled to the less developed regions of the
country, successive generations of common men were
forced to discard settled habits and fixed customs, to
break with family ties and old associations, and, relying
on their own initiative and common sense, to get along
with a minimum of governmental authority either to
assist or to restrain them. In few countries have the
common people been so little hampered in their
thought and conduct by tradition, or had so often to
adapt their lives to new and hazardous conditions, or
had so often an opportunity to follow the strong bent of
their spirits in devising fundamental constitutional laws
and new forms of government. This experience inevitably disposed them to minimize the function and authority of government and to emphasize, exaggerate if
you like, the liberty of the individual; that is to say, to

take it for granted that freedom of thought and conduct is the natural right of the individual, and that government, so far from being something transcendent and semidivine, is a homespun affair, a convenient committee appointed by them to perform certain communal services and in the nature of the case bound not to go beyond its instructions.

This conception of the function of government and the liberties of the individual was by no means acceptable to all classes in colonial times; but it was widely entertained in the eighteenth century, and the natural-rights political philosophy employed to justify the War of Independence raised it to the level of a universal principle. The natural-rights philosophy was of European origin. In the sixteenth century Protestant revolutionists appealed from the positive law to the higher law of God. In the seventeenth century English Puritan revolutionists appealed to the law of God and Nature. In the eighteenth century French and American revolutionists, reversing the order, appealed to the law of Nature and of Nature's God. Jefferson expressed what he called "the common sense of the subject" in the preamble of the Declaration of Independence, which may be reduced to four fundamental principles: (1) that the universe and man as a part of it are subject to natural law, which is God's revelation to men; (2) that all men have certain natural, that is to say, God-given rights; (3) that governments exist to secure these rights; and (4) that all just governments derive their authority from the consent of the governed.

The first premise of this philosophy is to be found in

the eighteenth-century conception of natural law. As understood by Jefferson and his contemporaries, natural law was never better defined perhaps than by the French philosopher Volney. Natural law, said Volney, is

that regular and constant order of facts by which God rules the universe; the order which his wisdom presents to the sense and reason of men, to serve them as an equal and common rule of conduct and to guide them, without distinction of race or sect, towards perfection and happiness.

The fundamental implication of this definition is that men, so far from being by nature prone to evil and error and for that reason incapable, apart from the compulsion of church and state, of arriving at the truth or living the good life, are endowed by God with reason in order that they may progressively discover that which is true, and with conscience in order that they may be disposed, in the measure of their enlightenment, to follow that which is good. If Jefferson and his contemporaries had a somewhat too optimistic faith in the natural goodness and intelligence of men, one reason is that they were living at a time when men had been and were being too much governed—a time when the obvious oppressions from which most men suffered were those imposed by the arbitrary authority of church and state. For that reason liberty could be most easily conceived in terms of the emancipation of the individual from social constraints, and the liberties which seemed essential at that time were those which had hitherto been most commonly denied—freedom of religion, freedom of speech and the press, freedom of occupation and economic enterprise, freedom from arbitrary government. These freedoms for the individual were precisely what Jefferson meant by "liberty" as one of the inalienable natural rights of man, and it was only by the fullest enjoyment of these rights that the "pursuit of happiness" would be most likely to result in the greatest happiness for the greatest number. And so we arrive at the central idea of the natural-rights philosophy in respect to the proper function of government and the liberties of the individual—the happy idea that the best way to secure the inalienable rights of man is just to leave men as free as possible to do what they please, and that no form of government can secure these rights so well as the one that governs least.

The natural-rights philosophy made its way in America with far less opposition than it did in Europe. It was adopted as a convenient theory for justifying separation from Great Britain; but with that end accomplished no further revolution of profound import, such as occurred in France, was required to bring the social and political institutions of the revolted colonies into substantial harmony with it. The federal and state constitutions were scarcely more than a codification of colonial institutions with the king and Parliament left out. Monarchical absolutism and the theory of divine right, the vested interests of an intrenched landed aristocracy resting on birth, the powerful influence of an established state church—none of these obstacles to political democracy, which had to be overcome in European countries, were ever in any real sense a part of our political tradition or practice. The people of the United States have never had to live under the shadow of a surviving ancient regime—have never, like the English, had to place a king in cold storage in order to keep a pretender off their backs; have never, like the French, had to make terms with powerful royalist and clerical parties openly or secretly bent on destroying the republic. The democratic political philosophy seems to them, as Jefferson said, merely the "common sense of the subject," and it seems to them the common sense of the subject because it is scarcely more than an ideological description of the institutions to which they have always been accustomed and to which they are devoted.

For our purpose the outstanding result of this happy blending of historical experience with the political philosophy that presided at the birth of the nation is that, since 1776 at least, the people of the United States have held, with singular unanimity, certain positive convictions about the essential meaning of political freedom. Political freedom, American style, means: (1) that the people are the ultimate source of all political power; (2) that the form of government is republican; and (3) that the powers of the government are precisely defined and limited in fundamental constitutional laws designed to safeguard the individual citizen against excessive or arbitrary power on the part of elected officials.

When the first constitutions were drafted, it was taken for granted that the governments should be republican—that is, government by representatives elected by the people; but as an afterthought, to make doubly sure, Article IV was inserted in the Federal

Constitution of 1789: "The United States shall guarantee to every State in this union a republican form of government." It was also taken for granted that the people are the source of all political power. Jefferson formulated the theory in the terse phrase: "Governments are instituted among men, deriving their just powers from the consent of the governed." The same theory, variously worded, is set forth in all our state constitutions, nowhere better perhaps than in the Texas constitution of 1845: "All political power is inherent in the people, and all free governments are founded on their authority and instituted for their benefit; and they have, at all times, the right to alter, reform, or abolish their government, in such manner as they may think expedient." Just who comprise the people in this sense (whether the people of the several states or of the United States) was much disputed, and a civil war had to be fought to decide the issue. But the main point is that since the founding of the Republic it has always been taken for granted, as a fundamental article in our political creed, that the people, however defined, have at all times the right to alter, reform, or abolish their government as they may think expedient.

But this right, although taken to be the foundation of political freedom, has never been thought to be the whole of it. If the people are to govern themselves, then obviously they must be the source of all political power. But the people are not one but many—many individuals and groups, with diverse and conflicting wills and interests. In a republic the only practical way of reconciling this conflict of wills and interests, the only way of determining the will of the people, is by majority vote. Jefferson accepted majority vote as a practical device, but he was not so naïve as to suppose that the majority would always be right or never be unjust. He believed that republican government, proceeding by majority vote, is the best safeguard against the tyranny of the one or the few; but he realized that there might easily be another sort of tyranny scarcely less oppressive—the tyranny of the majority.

Jefferson was not alone in this belief. His contemporaries agreed with him, and on the whole the people of the United States have always agreed with him. We accept the sovereignty of the people of necessity. Of necessity we trust the people as a whole to alter, reform, or abolish their government in such a manner as they may think expedient. But as individuals, impatient of restraints on our personal freedom to do and think as we like, we are a little afraid of the people as a whole, and we have always taken precautions against their going haywire. We have, as one may say, appealed from the people drunk with the possession of power to the people sobered by the fear of political oppression. And the interesting and significant result is that although no democratic nation is more entirely committed to the principle and practice of self-government proceeding by majority vote than we are, we have devised more, and more ingenious, ways of moderating, delaying, sidestepping, and hamstringing the will of the majority than any other democratic nation has thought it necessary or desirable to submit to.

13

The general over-all device for safeguarding our liberties against the shifting or ill-considered will of the majority is our system of written constitutions. The idea of a written constitution, defining the rights of citizens and the organization of government, acquired a high prestige in the eighteenth century because of the widespread belief that society could be deliberately and advantageously reconstructed according to a rational plan. The American Founding Fathers were not entirely uninfluenced by this idea, but the first American constitutions owed far less to political theory than to political experience. After the formal separation from Great Britain eleven of the states adopted state constitutions which were little more than revised editions of their respective colonial charters, while the other two, Rhode Island and Connecticut, were content to retain their charters as organic constitutions without any revision at all. The union of the states inevitably called for a federal constitution—first the ineffective Articles of Confederation, and then the Constitution of 1789. Subsequently, as each new state was admitted to the Union, the people of the state as a matter of course adopted a constitution for that state in all essentials similar to the ones with which they were familiar. There are now forty-eight states, and some of these have, from time to time, assembled constitutional conventions and adopted new constitutions in place of the old.

The French historian Taine made much of the fact that the French people had within a hundred years adopted as many as thirteen constitutions. But that was really nothing to write home about. He should have looked at Poore's collection of American constitutions which was published in 1878. There he would have found that within a hundred years after 1776 the people of the United States had adopted one hundred and four constitutions, with no assurance that the business would end there. Such fertility in constitution making would have astounded Taine, but we think nothing of it. The reason we think nothing of it is that in making a constitution we have never, since 1789, really had to think at all. All we have ever had to do is to copy, with some modifications in detail, the model created by the Founding Fathers—that is to say, a document which sets forth the familiar list of natural and imprescriptible rights of the citizen and provides for the organization of another republican government of the stereotyped pattern; a government in which the powers of elected representatives are precisely defined and strictly limited, carefully separated in respect to function, and otherwise rendered innocuous by applying the grand negative principle of checks and balances. Reading any of our numerous constitutions, one is so to speak transported into the eighteenth-century climate of opinion, and finds oneself contemplating political ideas and mechanisms admirably suited to sustain the professed faith of the Founding Fathers in the sovereignty of the people, and at the same time to abate their lively apprehension as to what might happen to political freedom if the people were ever permitted, except on infrequent and solemn occasions, to exercise that sovereignty without restraint.

The fundamental constitutional safeguard against

the unrestrained will of the people is defined in what are called the "bills of rights." Jefferson and his contemporaries believed that governments exist to secure the natural rights of men, but some of these rights they regarded as sacred and imprescriptible. They endeavored, therefore, to place them above and beyond the reach of legislative action by enumerating them in the constitutions and declaring them to be rights which no government could ever impair or deny. They were enumerated in the first state constitutions, and afterwards, without change in the content and with very little change in the phraseology, copied in all subsequent constitutions. All Americans are supposed to know them as they know the multiplication table, and do know them just about that well. They are (just in case some of them may have slipped from your memory) freedom of religion, freedom of speech and the press, freedom of assembly and the right to petition the government, freedom to bear arms in defense of the country, freedom of one's house and person from unwarranted search and seizure, freedom from the billeting of soldiers, freedom of private property from confiscation except for a public purpose and with adequate compensation, freedom from arbitrary arrest and imprisonment, the privilege of the writ of habeas corpus, the right to a speedy and public trial by a jury of one's peers, to subpoena witnesses, and to have legal assistance in one's defense, and freedom from bills of attainder, ex post facto laws, excessive fines, and cruel and unusual punishments.

In setting forth these civil liberties of the citizen, the

constitutions define a sphere of action which is entirely withdrawn from governmental control. But even within the sphere of action in which the government has authority the power of the government to act is subject to many limitations. The liberal-democratic revolution of the eighteenth century was directed primarily against those forms of government that permitted political power to be excessive, arbitrary, and concentrated. The Founding Fathers were therefore predisposed, both by political experience and the liberal-democratic political philosophy, to regard political power as inherently dangerous; and to their way of thinking the primary purpose of a written constitution was to devise a form of government in which political power would cease to be arbitrary and excessive by being strictly limited in scope, and cease to be concentrated by being carefully dispersed, checked, and balanced in its application.

I need not say that the Founding Fathers were eminently successful in achieving this object. In the form of government which they devised, and which in all essentials still exists, political power is dispersed, first of all, among the federal and state governments, according to the principle that "the powers not delegated to the United States by the Constitution, nor prohibited by it to the States, are reserved to the States respectively, or to the people." Within the federal and within each of the state governments, political power is further dispersed, according to the famous eighteenth-century principle of "separation of powers," among the executive, legislative, and judicial branches of the government; and for fear that any one branch might acquire

17

too much power within its own domain, each branch is further hampered by permitting the others to check its action under certain circumstances. Thus the executive cannot make laws, but it can veto laws made by the legislature. The legislature cannot execute laws, but it can hamper or nullify their execution by refusing to appropriate the money needed for that purpose. The courts can neither make laws nor execute them, but they can declare a law made and executed to be null and void if in their judgment it violates the constitution.

These are the chief ways in which political power is dispersed, checked, and balanced, but they are by no means the only ones. Money bills can originate only in the lower chamber, but have to be approved by the upper chamber; if so approved, they can then be vetoed by the executive, but then the two chambers can override the veto by a two-thirds majority. The treaty-making power is such that a treaty negotiated by the President and approved by the senators from thirty-one states, with a combined population of 125,000,000, can be vetoed by the senators from seventeen states with a combined population of less than 15,000,000. The electoral system is such that a man may become President of the United States although a majority of the voters have cast their ballots for someone else. The tenures of office are such that, under the two-party system, the executive may be controlled by one party, the legislative by the other. And the grand ironic result of all this is that we may, and often do, achieve an equilibrium of political power so perfectly balanced that movement, either forward or backward, is imperceptible because virtually nonexistent. In a system so effectively designed to frustrate and delay the will of the majority, the tyranny of the majority is indeed a remote contingency.

Such is the American conception of political freedom, and such the system of government designed to secure it. William Ewart Gladstone said that the Federal Constitution was the most remarkable political document ever struck off at a given time by the hand of man. It may be. At all events, our federal system, consisting of forty-nine governments, is certainly the most complicated, stable, toughly resistant, and impregnable political structure ever devised by any people. It is the American contribution to political science, and that it is an outstanding contribution cannot be denied. I at least do not know of any system of government, unless it be the English, that ever succeeded better in solving the fundamental problem of politics—the problem of the one and the many; of reconciling the desirable liberties of the individual with the necessary powers of society; of according to localities the maximum of self-government without enfeebling the state; of entrusting ultimate power to the people and at the same time safeguarding the rights of minorities. Nevertheless, admirable as the American constitutional system is, we need to remember that a system devised in the eighteenth century to meet the needs of thirteen sparsely populated agricultural communities on the Atlantic seaboard, at a time when it took Ben Franklin longer to travel from Philadelphia to New York than it now takes to fly bombing planes from New York to Hongkong, is not necessarily suited in all respects to the needs of the complex

19

and highly integrated technological society of the twentieth century.

We need to be reminded of this more especially because we have been rather too apt to regard our constitutions as revelations handed down from Mount Sinai —as documents which, since they set forth the universal principles of government, need never be re-examined. We think and speak of our liberties as "constitutional liberties"; and it may be said that we speak of them a great deal without thinking about them very much. It is as if in the eighteenth century we discovered and labeled our liberties, locked them safely away in oak-ribbed and riveted constitutions, placed the key under the mat, and then went cheerfully about our private affairs with a feeling of complete security. We have for the most part always felt that our civil liberties, even if we have forgotten just what they are, are safe because they are enumerated in the constitutions; and that our political freedom is safe because government is so bitted and bridled and hobbled by the constitutions that it can't run away with the wagon however loosely we hold the reins. From time immemorial men have been eager to believe that political authority is divinely ordained, and the system of written constitutions is our compensation for loss of faith in the divine right of kings. It is our rock of ages and our refuge. It gives us a sense of security and relieves us of responsibility. It enables us to gratify our respect for law, and at the same time to exhibit our contempt for laws, to revere the principle of liberty and at the same time to indulge our ingrained impulse to direct action. Throughout our history there run, side by side, the contrasted themes of conformity to law and lawlessness. Whether it be a matter of clearing the forest or exterminating the redskins, building railroads for the common good or rigging the market to milk them for private profit, establishing free schools by law or placing illegal restraints upon the freedom of teaching, conferring on Negroes their constitutional liberties or making sure they do not vote, declaring suspected persons to be innocent until proved guilty or subjecting them to the third degree, applauding the value of temperance or perceiving the convenience of bootlegging—whatever the immediate practical problem may be, we seem to act on the assumption that our freedoms, since they are so broad and secure, are expendable, and that we can take liberties with our liberty since it is so impregnably guaranteed. So long as the constitutions are not threatened, our liberties seem safe, manhandle them how we may.

Nothing discloses this characteristic attitude towards the Constitution more clearly than the debates occasioned by the conflict of interest between the North and the South prior to the Civil War. The fundamental issue, the issue which threatened and finally dissolved the Union, was the institution of slavery. Yet few people on either side, except the Abolitionists, were willing to mention slavery if it could be avoided: the harsh word "slavery" was softened down to "the peculiar institution." The sacred and inalienable rights of man, which Jefferson had made the foundation of all political freedom, were dismissed as "glittering generalities." The rights assumed to be fundamental were the positive rights guaranteed by the Constitution; and the prevailing assumption was that if only the correct interpretation of the Constitution could be found and agreed upon the difficulties occasioned by the "peculiar institution" would vanish and all would be well.

The legalistic attitude of mind reached its highest degree of refinement in the debates on the Compromise of 1850. In his speech of March 4, Calhoun asserted that "the agitation of the subject of slavery would, unless prevented by some timely and effective measure, end in disunion." This was as much as to say that the Union would be dissolved if the people insisted on discussing the institution that was in fact dissolving it. Webster, in his great Seventh of March speech, proceeded on essentially the same assumption. He appealed to the people, both North and South, to ignore the moral issue and to accept slavery as a local institution like any other—a peculiar institution perhaps, but one sanctioned by the Constitution and laws of the country. If, he said in effect, we will only take slavery for what it legally and constitutionally is, a species of property, and the fugitive slave as in the same category as a horse that has run away from its master and broken through a neighbor's fence—if, in short, we will only pretend that slavery is something else, we can keep slavery for those who want it and still have liberty and union for everyone.

Such was the prevailing view. There were exceptions. Many years before William Lloyd Garrison had declared that if the Constitution sanctioned slavery the Constitution was a covenant with death and a league

22

with hell. William H. Seward, in his speech on the Compromise, startled the country by declaring that "there is a higher law then the Constitution." James Russell Lowell illuminated the subject by saying that "to be told that we ought not to agitate the question of slavery, when it is that which is forever agitating us, is like telling a man with the fever and ague on him to stop shaking, and all will be well." And Lincoln, disregarding the advice of all his friends, forecast the future by declaring that a house divided against itself could not stand, that the Union could not endure half slave and half free and would inevitably become all one thing or all the other.

In 1850 the Union was already so effectively divided in spirit that it was then too late to make the only compromise that could have been effective and advantageous to both South and North—voluntary emancipation of the slaves by the Southern states, and compensation to the slaveowners by the federal government. Passions ran so high that a doorkeeper in the House of Representatives could not be chosen without making sure he would not agitate the subject of slavery. It is not strange then that the Compromise of 1850 left the "irrepressible conflict" precisely where it was. One concession to the South was the repeal of the Wilmot Proviso, although it was admitted on both sides that the North would gain nothing by retaining the Proviso, the South nothing by its repeal. The principal concession to the South was the Fugitive Slave Act, a measure strenuously demanded, not by the border states whose slaves could easily escape to the North, but by the states in the deep South whose slaves could not. There was already a fugitive slave act which worked well enough. The new one, besides being a violation of the Federal Constitution, was so offensive to the North that it could not be enforced; and its only practical effect was to increase and embitter the discussion of slavery instead of putting an end to it. The Compromise of 1850 was a futile effort to solve a fundamental question of human rights and property interests by appealing to legal rules and precedents and making concessions on points of no substantial importance—concessions to wounded pride and lost prestige and constitutional rights that conferred no advantage. It may have postponed the Civil War for a few years, but it certainly did nothing to prevent it. It was in effect a compromise to end all compromises.

We are now in the midst of another critical period in our history. The house is again in the way of being divided. The division is not now between people living in different geographical regions, but between people living on different levels in respect to possessions and opportunities. But this division, like the last one, concerns the rights of men and the interests of property. The problem may be stated as follows: How can we bring about, through the system of private economic enterprise, that degree of equality of possessions and of opportunity without which democracy is no more than an empty form, and at the same time preserve those freedoms of the individual in the intellectual and political realm without which democracy cannot exist? We will not solve that problem by Seventh of March speeches, by appealing to the people to refrain from "agitating" the institution of private economic enterprise, which is in fact the central issue. Above all, we will not solve it by resting in the comfortable conviction that our freedoms are secure because they are enumerated and defined in the constitutions. The time is past when we could afford to take politics lightly as an amusing game played for low stakes. We need now, as the Founding Fathers did in 1787, to give serious thought to the fundamentals of politics; and perhaps the first step in that direction would be to unlock our eighteenth-century constitutions and examine with some care what is therein contained in the light of the problems raised by the complex technological society of our time.

If we did that, certain disturbing questions would inevitably arise—questions concerning our civil liberties and questions concerning the structure of our government. For example, freedom of speech is an invaluable right and must be preserved, but does it necessarily include the right to publish scandal sheets and exploit the misfortunes of families, to employ corporations and fruity-throated radio announcers to misinform some of the people all of the time about the merits of commodities made and sold for private profit? Is freedom of speech compatible with laws permitting postmasters to refuse mailing privileges to publications which they may think uneducational, frivolous, or indecent? The right of persons charged with crime to a speedy and fair trial is an invaluable right, but is trial by jury as now conducted, which proceeds on the assumption that if two sets of skilled lawyers distort the facts in opposite directions the truth will emerge, the best method of securing that right?

It is obvious that our civil liberties could be made somewhat more secure by rephrasing our bills of rights in the light of modern conditions. That could be done if we had only one constitution. The difficulty is that we have forty-nine constitutions, and if any substantial change is made in either the phrasing or content of one bill of rights, the same changes should be made simultaneously in all of them; otherwise our civil liberties might vary from state to state as much as our divorce laws do, and come to be regarded with the same levity and derision. It is probably a sound instinct on the part of the people to feel that it is dangerous to meddle with our bills of rights, and legislation is probably the best method of approach for securing our civil liberties more effectively; but it is equally dangerous to feel that our civil liberties are secure because they are set forth in all our constitutions in the same archaic and consecrated phrases. If the civil liberties are in form and spirit denied every day to someone, and no one bothers about it unless he is that someone, less than nothing is gained by pointing out that they are specifically enumerated and properly defined in forty-nine constitutions and may be defended in the courts.

If we examine the structure of our government, other and even more important questions arise. It is desirable to have a system in which the rights of minorities are protected, but is it desirable to have those rights so well protected that minorities can, for the promotion of class or local interest or private profit, so easily block or side-step legislation designed for the protection of the majority? It is desirable to confer on local communities the maximum of self-government in matters of purely local interest, but is it desirable to have a system in which the local communities are so arbitrarily delimited that the map of the United States looks like a cardboard puzzle, and in which many of the powers reserved to these communities have become, since they were so reserved, of national rather than of purely local importance? It is desirable to have checks on the concentration and abuse of political power, but is it desirable to have power so checked and channeled and dispersed that no body of representatives elected to assume the responsibilities of government can be held clearly responsible for any policies adopted or any measures passed? In short, would it not be desirable (and this is the most important question that arises in connection with the structure of our government) to have a system in which political power and political responsibility are more united, more clearly defined and placed, and more responsive to the clearly expressed will of the nation?

This question is of long standing. Walter Bagehot in *The English Constitution* (1867), Woodrow Wilson in *Congressional Government* (1885), James Bryce in *The American Commonwealth* (1888), and more recently Henry Hazlitt in *A New Constitution Now* (1942) have pointed out with remarkable clarity those defects of the American system of government which derive from the separation of powers and the staggered election of magistrates for fixed terms. The defects boil down to three principal ones: (1) Neither the President nor the Congress can formulate and carry through a policy if the other objects. (2) In case of conflict between the President and the Congress, there is no way of referring the issue to the electorate for decision until the next election, when very likely the issue has been forgotten or merged in other issues. (3) Elections cannot be held merely because there is something important to be decided, but must be held in certain years whether there is anything important to be decided or not. As Bagehot said, "You have bespoken your government in advance, and whether it suits you or not, whether it works well or ill, whether it is what you want or not, by law you must keep it." Nothing can unmake a President, as Woodrow Wilson acridly put it, "except four successions of the seasons. . . . A Prime Minister must keep himself in favor with the majority, a President need only keep alive." Packing the essence of the matter in one phrase—"division of authority and concealment of responsibility"—Wilson pointed out that the lack of authority to decide when some decision is called for is a weakness at all times, "but in times of sudden exigency it might prove fatal—fatal in breaking down the system or in failing to meet the emergency." [1] In other countries which have adopted the principle of separation of powers—in France in 1852 and in 1939, in most South American republics at various times—the system has broken down. That it has not broken down

---

[1] The quotations are taken from Henry Hazlitt's *A New Constitution Now* (New York, 1942), pp. 27, 29–31.

28

in the United States is due partly to the fact that great emergencies have been rare and partly to the political genius and self-restraint of the people.

There are those who say that we should remedy these defects by "adopting" the British system of cabinet government and ministerial responsibility. If this means that we should take over the British system wholesale, I do not agree, not because the British system is not an excellent one, but because political systems cannot, like motor cars and illuminated manuscripts, be imported with any assurance that they will retain their original value. Political institutions, to be effective and stable, must be firmly grounded on the political traditions and habitual ways of thinking of the people who establish them. If, then, we need a form of government in which power and responsibility are more united, more definitely placed, and more responsive to the will of the nation, we must work it out for ourselves, within the framework of our traditional system of written constitutions, by a modification of the basic principle of separation of powers—that is to say, by bridging the gulf which now separates the executive and the legislative branches and permits them, even in times of emergency when great issues are at stake, to work at cross-purposes, to advocate diverse and conflicting policies, to indulge in mutual recrimination, and at worst to debase the business of government to the level of a disingenuous contest for popular support at the next election.

The direct and deliberate way to bridge this gulf is by a revision of the Federal Constitution. Theoretically this is always possible; and practically it is not difficult, although much time is required, to amend the Constitution whenever the people want it amended. When the people wanted a federal income tax, national women's suffrage, and prohibition, the Constitution was amended with little difficulty; when they got tired of prohibition, it was unamended with even less difficulty. But no amendment so far has touched the basic structure of government; and at present there is no popular demand for a modification of the principle of separation of powers, or even any widespread realization that it is not essential to the maintenance of the republican form of government. At present, therefore, a revision of the Constitution is impossible because the people do not want it. But I believe that sooner or later the complex conditions of modern society will make it necessary to find some means of inducing the White House and Capitol Hill to abandon the competitive struggle for occupying the limelight and avoiding responsibility, and to assume a joint responsibility for framing coherent policies and carrying them into effect. In a world loaded with social dynamite we cannot go on forever muddling through with a system of government so effectively designed for passing the buck.

A distinguished economist, the late H. J. Davenport of Cornell University, once said that the law is the only discipline that has a backward outlook on the progress of mankind. To think that our liberties are secure because they are abstractly defined and constitutionally guaranteed is to have this backward outlook. It is to mistake the legal form for the living substance of political freedom. To have a government of laws is indeed necessary, but to suppose that because we have a government of laws we have not a government of men is a misleading and dangerous fallacy. Any government, even a government of laws, is never better than the men who administer it; and in a republican government, if the people through ignorance, indifference, and dishonesty, renounce their individual and collective responsibility for the preservation of freedom, the laws, whether constitutional or other, will not do it for them.

When the Constitutional Convention of 1787 finished its labors, a certain Mrs. Powell of Philadelphia asked Benjamin Franklin: "Well, Doctor, what have we got, a Republic or a Monarchy?" Franklin replied: "A Republic, *if you can keep it.*" We still have our republic. We still have our political freedoms. But the question still is, can we keep them? We can keep them if we are willing to pay the price. The price, I think, is to take politics more seriously than we have usually done or needed to do. If we are willing to examine the fundamentals of politics once more with as much care as the Founding Fathers did, and can display as much intelligence and wisdom in adapting our political institutions to the complex political problems of our time as they did to the problems of their time, we can undoubtedly keep our republic and the liberties that are essential to it. We might in that case do even more than that—we might conceivably make another outstanding contribution to political science.

31

FREEDOM:
IMAGE AND REALITY

BY MAX LERNER

An Editor of PM

"MEN LIVE BY SYMBOLS,"
we have been told; and it is a deep truth, provided only that the symbol stands for something that is substance and not sham. So it is with freedom, and that body of freedoms which Americans call their "civil liberties." We often pay homage to our Revolutionary Fathers as the authors of our freedom, and with a graceful word for their living and dying and a sigh for their memories, we dismiss the whole subject. But those men who fought to be free men did not fight for a word or a memory. They fought for a present image in their hearts, which had been given a living reality by hardship and bloodshed and the experience of a new continent.

What was the source of that image? It is often called the "American dream," yet I venture to say that it was far more the imprint of the European dream on the American reality. That dream took many forms—as anyone knows who has studied the intellectual history of the seventeenth and eighteenth centuries. It was the child of God showing his faith by works, the good husbandman seeking to cultivate not only his garden but his soul, the fearless sailor finding his Utopia in an imaginary voyage, the seeker after Nature's essence who finds it finally away from the corruptions of "civilization," the Plutarchian hero transposed into eighteenth-century Europe who dies with courage because he has lived for his community, the paradoxical fellow who worships Nature but studies her laws of motion so that he may tame her and out of that taming grow rich and great. Dr. Faustus was part of that composite European dream, and Francis Bacon, and Jean Jacques Rousseau; Candide and Robinson Crusoe, and the Greek tyrannicides. Professor Becker has named that dream better than anyone else when he called it the "heavenly city."

Without the "heavenly city" the image of American freedom would have been impossible. The European brought his dream to the American soil. It is in the nature of a dream to be spun in imagination by those who cannot enact it in their waking life. The European went through feudalism and the agony of meaningless wars; he lived through religious persecutions; he knew tyrants and priestly hierarchies; crowded into a small compass, tilling an often exhausted soil, he generated an earth hunger that never left him; he saw the rainbow of limitless profit only to be denied it by iron mercantilist restrictions on his enterprise. He lived, in short, in what had become in effect a closed society. In America the soil was rich; the restrictions were gone; there was a direct relation between a man's effort and his reward; and—whether illusion or not—one had the sense of starting with an institutional clean slate. A man could stand up. The deepest element in the American image of freedom was the consciousness of the difference between the closed society of an old culture and the open society of a new one.

That consciousness has never been wholly erased from the American mind. Remember that America is a cultural deposit left by successive waves of immigration. There can be little quarrel with the classic Turner stress on the importance of the sustained frontier in keeping alive men's sense of the possible; but one must add to it the importance of sustained immigration in keeping alive men's yearning to stretch the bounds of the possible. And while it is fashionable to praise the earlier waves of immigration at the expense of those which came later, one must note that the latest immigration of all is that of men and women who wear the image of freedom closest to their hearts because they have seen freedom crumpled beneath a fascist tank, and have seen also the miracle of its rising again to destroy its destroyer.

Here, then, is the American image of freedom. But an image can also be a sword, and this one was forged in the unsettlement of Europe and the settlement of America, tempered in the great tempering crises of the national existence—the Revolution, the Civil War, the World Wars—given a sheath to wear in the code of the Bill of Rights, kept sharp in its cutting edge by the renewing dreams of the young generations both native and immigrant, and by the struggles waged by nameless men and women against the powers and principalities of darkness.

37

I do not use the figure of the sword as a rhetorical flourish. The deepest experience of men has shown that either the desire for freedom is a militant and passionate thing or it is nothing. And let me add that any image which moves millions of men to action and passion must be more even than a burning desire. I borrow the phrase of Alexander Meiklejohn, from his too neglected book *What Does America Mean?* where you will find that to be effective freedom must be both desire and commitment. And here I touch on one of the most vulnerable aspects of American life when I say that while the desire for freedom has by no means slackened, the commitment to freedom has not kept pace with that desire. How many times during the past terrible decade of the world's history have we heard it said that the struggles for freedom elsewhere in the world were no concern of Americans? How many times within our own country has freedom been interpreted as the freedom to wreak one's own economic power upon another's economic helplessness? How many times has the tradition of the American frontier and its individualism been called upon to justify not the freedom of the frontier (which was the freedom of men who valued it because they clung together in a precarious community), but the predacity of the jungle?

When we think of freedom in these latter days we are as likely as not to think of the freedom we want for ourselves, rather than the freedom we are committed to extending to others and the price we are willing to pay for that commitment. I weigh my words carefully when

38

I say that while the desire for freedom has in some ways grown, the commitment to it has lessened.

This, if it is indeed a fact, is part of what I call the reality of freedom. Let us look more closely at that reality. The tensions of politics, the tenacities of corporate power, the bewildering impact of an expanding world, the flux of institutional forms, and the influx of new and strange idea patterns are greater today than ever in American culture. And freedom as a reality may seem a tenuous thing buffeted about between these forces.

To get a long perspective on this, we have only to compare our own America with the America of Andrew Jackson's day, roughly a century ago. I use that as a point of reference not only because it was the seed ground of our present-day big industrialism, before the seeds had flowered, but also because it was the period of what Professor Matthiessen has called the "American Renaissance." For it was the time when Emerson was spinning Platonic dreams but also living them with a New England passion, when Hawthorne was seeking to fathom the nature of guilt and Melville pursuing the white whale of evil.

Compared with that day our own has seen cultural changes that go to freedom's core. The farm as a working and living unit has been replaced by the factory as a working unit and the city as a living unit. People live and work closer together; this begets new tolerances, but also new animosities. A new dependence has set in. The ordinary man—factory worker, white-collar worker, farmer—has become separated from the ownership of soil and tools, and from the sense he once had that, come what might, he would somehow get along. He is uprooted, propertyless, dependent on vast impersonal aggregates of power for his own slender security.

The home-as-control has been loosened. So also, for a large part, has the church-as-control. The school-as-control, afflicted in most communities and many colleges with a suicidal timidity in the face of controversial issues, has abdicated its critical function of community leadership. The new opinion agencies which might have assumed this function—the Big Press, the Chain Radio, the Mass Movies—have not done so, both from economic interest and moral cowardice. And without an active leadership in the fight against the forces of unfreedom, the reality of freedom cannot thrive.

There were many who thought that it would be wholly snuffed out by the war. The striking thing about civil liberties under World War II, as compared with World War I, is that although the present war comes closer to being a total war, there has been less actual repression of liberties by public governments, whether federal or state. One recalls that during the Great Debate before Pearl Harbor there were warnings, based no doubt on the experience of the "deadly parallel," that if we entered a total war for freedom, our own freedom would be extinguished and we would become totalitarian. Thus far that has not happened, either in

England or America, and the prophets today stand shivering in all the nakedness of doom unfulfilled—a fact that may well serve as a primary datum for future political theorists to mull over, and to extract from it what grave conclusions they can about democracy, war, and freedom.

My own tentative guess is that the relative freedom from state repression—in the sense in which the thousands of arrests and convictions and prison terms during World War I constituted state repression—is due in equal parts to a sadder and wiser federal government and to a less critical attitude toward the war on the part of radical opinion. The government is sadder because the Department of Justice has been made wary by what it did in World War I. The government is wiser because President Roosevelt has a Holmesian skepticism that Wilson lacked. As the whole Debs episode showed, Wilson—being an idealist—hugged his resentments implacably to his breast, whereas Roosevelt has a saving sense of humor and flexibility.

But it must be added that he is less sorely beset than Wilson was by the liberals and the radicals. For this has from the beginning been a liberal's antifascist war as well as a war for the conservative's survival. And since the entrance of Russia, even the Communists have adhered to the war, after a period of bitter opposition during which the impact of their hostility was felt in the industries turning out armaments for the Allies, and they in turn felt the impact of the government's hostility in the Browder and other prosecutions. Had the radicals opposed the war after Pearl Harbor, it is a safe guess that the government's remarkable record on free speech might not have been much better in World War II than it was in World War I. Since it is mainly the reactionary isolationists and the fascists who oppose the war, and since those who sit at the strategic passes of American opinion have shown how little sympathy they have for calling them to account, only a hundred people have been sent to prison for sedition as compared with thousands in World War I.

But this record cannot be matched in another area of state action. As more liberty has been allowed for wartime speech, more surveillance has been imposed on thought and activity. The result is a surveillance or dossier state in which can be found the beginnings of the police state.

One of the curious paradoxes of freedom is that it should be the rise of new ideas which makes things unhealthy for the free discussion of any ideas. The big ideological specter of our time (I call it by its doctrinal name) is socialism. It continues to haunt the men of power in a community even during a war against fascism which is, whatever its pretensions, the bitterest enemy of the socialist idea. And it is, I think, largely out of fear of this idea—curiously enough, by a government that is often called socialist—that we are seeing the beginnings of the surveillance state in America.

The central instrument of the surveillance state is a political police, operating with both secrecy and efficiency, as the crucial arm of the existing structure of social power. This is true whether you are speaking of

Joseph Fouché's work in organizing Napoleon's police and espionage system, or the work of the Okhrana in Czarist and of the GPU in Soviet Russia, or of that most ruthless and nihilist of all police institutions, the Nazi Gestapo. To a greater or lesser degree this form of political policing has been characteristic of every state which has not cherished a strong image of freedom— what we call the civil liberties tradition. It has been the rule rather than the exception in the world's political history, just as liberty has been the exception rather than the rule.

One of the healthiest and most striking things about England and America, as contrasted with the tradition both of the European continent and the Orient, has been the absence of a political police. But it would have been a miracle if something of the temper of a political police had not, during the past quarter century, infiltrated even into our culture. The hunt for radicals and pacifists during the first World War, for radicals among aliens after the war, for racketeers and highjackers and kidnapers during the lamentable period of Prohibition provided the basis for a brilliant machine of federal policing, with exactly the elements of mid-twentieth-century efficiency which could be turned to the tasks of political surveillance. A crucial step was taken when Congress, in passing the 1940 Alien Registration Act, imposed on the federal enforcing agencies the broad task of curbing subversive utterances. Being a peacetime sedition measure, the first in our history for a century and a half, it called for machinery and powers beyond what might be necessary to deal with overt acts

43

of sabotage and actual conspiracy with the enemy.

This has meant a dossier on every writer and commentator in the country, every teacher of prominence, every trade-union official. And so we get many of the accouterments of the Continental police tradition—the secret agents, the police dossier, the secret and often stupid inquiries, the classifying and pigeonholing of men and women in a way that may hamper their movements, affect their jobs and careers, even blast their lives, on the basis of inquiries over which they have no check or chance for correction and counterevidence. Supplementing this system of controlling Dangerous Thoughts is a system of alien registration, immigration and emigration control, deportation machinery, enemy alien control, passport control, postoffice censorship, and government job surveillance.

In the latter area especially, but also in the others, we must recognize that we are dealing not only with administrative enforcement agencies—with which we associate the hated term "bureaucrats"—but also with Congress, which coruscates in our political literature as the tribune of the people and the palladium of the people's liberties. One of the most startling manifestations of the police state in our time is the campaign of terror against liberal government officials, taking the form of Congressional purges of federal employees, against whom have been leveled charges of disloyalty and un-Americanism. This is a topic which it may be superfluous of me to discuss at Cornell because Professor Cushman has written of it with that combination of scrupulousness and courage which is his mark. I call it startling because there has been nothing like it in the history of the American Republic; because it has operated irresponsibly and even unconstitutionally; because it has ignored the elementary judicial decencies; because it shows how legislative terrorism can function in the shadow world of political surveillance.

This may sound harsh; I mean it to be just. I am speaking of the entire record of the House Committee to Investigate Un-American Activities. I am speaking of its now famous campaign against the Thirty-Nine, begun in Congress in February, 1943, whose anabasis has not yet found its adequate Xenophon; I am speaking of the effort to pass a bill of attainder through the expedient of attaching a rider to an appropriation bill precluding the payment of any funds to specific persons, thus using the power of the purse to achieve wholly unfiscal purposes; I am speaking of the vague and confused definition of what is subversive, on the basis of which the dismissal of devoted public servants was recommended; I am speaking of the instilling of fear into the hearts of tens of thousands of other public officials who felt that they might at any moment be denounced and dismissed, and both their names and careers infected with an ineradicable taint. If their situation were not so tragic, there would be elements of high comedy in it—elements that might form the material for a great satire on wartime Washington, if we could find someone with the satiric gifts that Ignazio Silone showed in *Fontamara*.

It is clear that all the functions of surveillance and control that I have mentioned must be carried on to a degree in a wartime state. It is just as clear that they can be grossly abused even in a wartime state, and that they have little place in a peacetime state. In some of them you have a corruption of the administrative process, in others of the legislative process. What ties them all together is that they are directed toward the intangibles of political opinion. This is the surveillance state *in esse;* it is the police state *in posse.* Even in the right hands it casts a long shadow; in the wrong hands it could stifle opinion and break down liberty completely. Unfortunately no one is ever in position to know whether the power is in the wrong or right hands, and it may be doubted whether one may speak of such a thing as the "right hands" where wholly arbitrary power is concerned. Its operations are secret. Even efficiency, that demigod whom machine-minded Americans worship as the Greeks worshiped Dionysus and Pan, is no form of insurance. For the use of precision techniques and the latest technology, let us say by the Federal Bureau of Investigation, is at its best only when applied to the tangibles of crime detection. In the area of ideas such a technology is a rough intruder, like Caliban in a library. In the area of ideas freedom thrives best and is most creative when ideas are less sedulously policed.

I want to turn now, in our survey of the realities of freedom, from governmental action to the mass mind. In the governmental area almost all the surveillances are directed toward liberal and radical opinion. But in the area of mass violence and terrorism, it is fascist attitudes and propaganda that are predominant. And moving from one to the other, it is as if one were moving from a synthetic world to an actual one, from the fabricated dangers of liberal opinion to the quick blood spilled by fascist terrorism, from a world of fantasy to the rediscovery of the reality principle.

I speak of terrorism advisedly, for what has developed during the years over which Hitler's shadow hung has been the beginnings of mass vigilantism, in the name of the fascist principle of racial inferiority and superiority. I refer to a three-pronged attack. First, the anti-Negro and anti-Mexican riots from California to New York, from Beaumont to Detroit; and with those riots the whole practice of discrimination against Negroes, in jobs, in the armed services and army camps, in educational opportunity. Second, I refer to the hoodlum terrorism against Jewish children, along with the whole practice of anti-Jewish discrimination and anti-Jewish feeling which has substantially increased since Nazism became a serious factor in world opinion some fifteen or twenty years ago. And third, there is the west coast hysteria against Japanese-Americans—not only in their forced evacuation from their homes and their segregation in relocation centers, but also in the continued incitements of violence against them if they should seek to return to their homes after the war. I have no comment on the treatment of the Japanese enemy aliens; the nationals of an enemy are clearly subject to rigorous wartime controls. But I have been dismayed at the similar treatment accorded to American citizens, where the only basis for discrimination as

47

against citizens of German or Italian descent is pigmentation and cranial structure.

In the face of this three-pronged campaign of mass terrorism after a racist pattern, there is a grim meaning to be attached to the passivity of American opinion. This applies, may I say, to North as well as South, to the east coast as well as the west coast, to urban and rural areas alike. It applies to church and school and press, to large sections of labor as to industry, to the small businessman as well as to the major areas of Big Management and Big Property. If these were offenses against property, as in the case of the sit-down strikes of 1937, what an outcry would already have been raised against them in Congress and the press. They are, however, only threats against personal liberty and human decency, which may count for much less in an acquisitive society where a respectable status can be translated into money terms, a society also, may I add, where respectability depends on not being in any way identified with the minority groups who are being pushed around in accord with the dominant prejudices of the community. Possibly also this passivity may be the expression of a people with a deep subconscious racism of its own, and a people whose capacity to react to crimes against liberty of the person has been numbed by a decade of ruthless fascist terrorism and war all over the world.

But it would be a mistake to attribute the lack of popular commitment to civil liberties wholly to racist impulses. Part of the context, at least, is economic; and to that I now turn.

Let us remember that we have moved in the past century from an agrarian economy in which the pursuit of freedom was arduous but not heroic, to a machine economy and a Big Property society where the still, small voice of freedom is often drowned out by the deafening noise of the machines and the tones of authority with which economic power speaks.

Thorstein Veblen used to say in his books that the "unremitting discipline of the machine process" would some day establish an engineering society, and that the machine was undermining what he called the "animistic" or, as we should now say, authoritarian and nonrational elements in our institutions. The animistic images he had in mind were those of unequal property and economic power. But he tended to forget that freedom too is first of all an image in the mind before it can become a reality in society; that it cannot be defended in terms of weight and count and measure, or of personal utilitarianism, but only as it is a primary value in a hierarchy of values. Nor did he see clearly enough that before the ultimate effects of the machine wiped away the social inequalities on which unfreedom thrives, the immediate effects of the machine, at least under the control of Big Property, would be to undermine freedom rather than to strengthen it.

For the few, economic freedom consists of what they call a "free enterprise economy"—that is, freedom of corporate management from community control. But for the many, economic freedom means the freedom of the job—that is, equality of bargaining power, and freedom for the trade-union to become Big Unionism side by side with Big Management. And here the paradox enters. In order to achieve the equality of bargaining position at which, as Mr. Justice Holmes once put it, freedom of contract begins, the struggle to build up strong trade-unions has roused antilabor feeling on the part of agrarian and middle-class groups, powerfully abetted by Big Management and by the Big Press and the Chain Radio which express its viewpoint. It is this antilabor feeling which furnishes the context of industrial violence, in which labor's organizing efforts clash not only with company police and provocateurs, but also with community resistance. And it is this antilabor feeling which furnishes the context for the resistance to the enforcement of labor laws, as in the Montgomery Ward case, and for the violations of freedom on the job.

One can find a similar paradox in the question of full employment. It can scarcely be doubted that unless, after this war, we get something approaching full employment, the struggle to maintain freedom and an attitude of mutual tolerance and social decency will require nothing short of social heroism. But here again the paradox enters. Full employment is essential to freedom. But, given the concentration of economic power, the steps that are necessary to achieve full employment will also meet with powerful resistances which will make freedom precarious. I know of no credible body of economic thought which believes that full employment can be achieved without strong fiscal or planning controls, or both. Yet it is hard to see how those controls can be organized without raising again the specters of ideological radicalism, and along with them the forces of repression.

A similar paradox will be found in the international economic situation. The United States cannot legislate postwar prosperity in a world vacuum. We shall need to lend technological skills and extend financial credits to other countries—both to create foreign markets for our own products, and also on the principle that there is an interdependence between expanding economies and that our own economy cannot expand unless other economies are also moving toward higher wages and higher living standards. But if the governments of Europe and Asia move toward social democracy, the project of extending large credits to them and exchanging technological skills is again likely to encounter heavy resistance and be exploited by the extremist fascist elements in our own country.

That means that the great malady of our time is the tropism of contraction in the midst of forces crying out for expansion. I am thinking now of a closed society as a society which is in danger of losing some of its original dynamic, whose economic rulers have grown fearful of their power, whose channels for the expression of competing ideas have grown constricted, and whose intellectual universe is therefore narrowing. When these forces go far enough, you get the closed society—or, to use John Stuart Mill's famous phrase from another context in the famous chapter of the *Principles of Political*

Economy, the "Stationary State." Freedom does not thrive in a state with hermetically sealed frontiers, shrunken perspectives, and a closed mind.

America has not been immune to the malady, which has to a far greater degree affected most other peoples. This nation, which was made by the inpouring of human streams from all over the world, now doles out immigration quotas with the most fearful chariness. The people who offered asylum to the oppressed, wherever they might come from, have now virtually closed their doors against the refugees from Hitler's tyranny, with the prospect that after the war even the thin stream that has thus far been allowed will be shut off. A nation which has grown powerful through its technology, and has almost made a cult of the know-how, denies to skilled men a chance to use their skills because of their color. In a nation that has grown great through education, strong forces fight the efforts of the government to make teaching and books and laboratories accessible through federal aid to every region, income group, population stratum. In a nation whose very lifeblood is the circulation of ideas, the opinion industries have become mechanized and monopolized like any other, and the circulation of the blood has become so controlled that it is pumped by mechanical hands through a mechanical heart. Every day there are fewer newspapers in the country, with an even tighter control of the channels of majority opinion by an ever smaller minority. Every day the powerful broadcasting chains, linked in their interest and their opinions with the owning groups of the country, use their strategic position to narrow the range of permitted ideas. Competition fares as badly in the market of ideas as in any other. This constriction of ideas should be the gravest concern for a free people. For freedom can die as effectively from exhaustion of the air in a closed chamber as from a dagger thrust by an avowed enemy.

The basic impetus for this constriction of opinion comes from the fears of an owning group fighting for privilege and position in the face of the controls necessary for an expanding economy. If we have in the years following the war the same disuse of men and machines and capital that we had in the decade preceding the war, it will mean an economy contracting because of the inability of its masters to widen their perspective through the nation's experience.

I submit that the Old Conservative of our time is a surrounded man. Like an Emperor Jones in a jungle, he lives in a terrible fantasy world, fearing enemies that he cannot see because they do not exist. He has become the victim of a paranoid delusion, the victim of a myth of encirclement.

I call it that because, in political history, the form that deep fears have always taken is the sense of being encircled by enemies. Perhaps that is an inheritance from the centuries of wilderness living and tribal isolation through which mankind has passed, and of which the nation-state that Arnold Toynbee has called the "parochial state" is only the latest expression.

What do the American economic rulers fear as their encircling enemies? They fear new and radical ideas, they fear the growing strength of labor, they fear controls by a popularly elected government; above all else, they have the sense that the world outside is in the throes of revolution, that dangerous forces have been unleashed in Europe and Asia. They conclude that if we can build a wall against them, if we can keep them from invading our shores, and if we can stamp out the ideas that have already infiltrated inside the wall, our movers and shakers can rule in peace. Hence their identification of liberal ideas with foreign doctrine, of aliens with radicalism, of labor with aliens, and of Communism with any thought that breaks the hard crust of habit.

That this is largely a world of delusion is attested by the plain experience of recent years. The inertia of institutions and the tenacities of habit are so great that there has never been a threat of a proletarian revolution in America. The threats from within are only threats from the shadows cast by the fears themselves.

One can easily discern how delusive are the fears of the business community that capitalism—what they now call with an unconscious irony the "free enterprise system"—is being threatened from without. There has never been a time during the past seventy-five years when opinion from right to left, including even the new Communist party line, has been more agreed than now on the proposition that capitalism has to be made to work, and that it can, if wisely handled, yield an economy of full employment. But the psychiatrists tell us that it is useless to reassure a man suffering from delusions of persecution: every reassurance serves only to confirm his initial fears.

This myth of encirclement leads logically to witch-hunting within a nation, and to militarist and imperialist adventures without. In the measure that the fearful men grow panicky of the liberal state, they call upon it in the name of encirclement to set up a watch and ward over dangerous thoughts. In fact, the very people who most violently protest against a Domesday Book of entries of wealth, income, wages, profits are the people who are most passionately in favor of a Domesday Book of entries of ideas and their professors.

What applies to the emergence of the police state applies also to the imperialist thrust. There is nothing incompatible between a sense of encirclement and imperialism. W. H. Auden has, with shrewd insight, called Rudyard Kipling the poet of encirclement. And it is true that as the English ruling class grew more convinced of the white man's danger before the yellow and black perils, it grew also more convinced of the need for the white man's burden. As the German ruling class failed to resolve its internal problems, it too became obsessed with the idea of encirclement by Jews and Bolsheviks; and it is notable that German culture produced not only an Alfred Rosenberg but also an Oswald Spengler, whose *Hour of Decision* is a hysterical warning against the yellow peril. Even in Russia, the myth of capitalist encirclement was largely responsible for the purges, the treason trial, and the rigor of a one-party system. And we in America may yet discover in our own country that witch-hunting isolationism and imperialism are brothers under the skin, and that we shall not medicine ourselves to democratic health until our ruling group has faced its fears and seen that they are not flesh but fantasy.

Postwar America will be a country of men habituated to the practice of violence and the techniques of military obedience. It will be a country in which the dichotomy between soldiers and civilians will be a new and great source of friction. It will be a country in which there will be millions of men accustomed to the sense of power, and frustrated without it. This is not a social context in which we can expect the sensitive plant of freedom to take care of itself.

What aid can we give it? There are those who say that the crux of freedom is the individual, and that only a return to individualism—economic and moral—will solve the problems of civil liberties.

I agree that the individual is the core of the whole problem of civil liberties. It is for the individual and his dignity that freedom exists: without him it has no meaning. But though freedom exists for the individual alone, it cannot be achieved by the individual alone. That is the nub of the matter, so far as civil liberties are concerned. There must be freedom *for* the individual. But it can be achieved only by the machinery of community action—whatever may be necessary to accomplish full employment in an expanding economy, equality of bargaining power and of economic and educational opportunity, protection to the religious conscience of each group.

But even this community machinery is not enough. Freedom is not freedom unless it is cemented by a sense

56

of society. I use "society" now in the sense of the comradeship and the organic interdependence of men. In fact, I suspect that the history of Greek and American individualism would show that in both cases the freedom of the individual came to be celebrated in a community which was certain of the ties between individuals. I maintain that the sense of society comes first—without it freedom becomes impossible. You cannot start by being anarchs and end as brothers; you must first have a sense of the basic decency of man to man before you can have a freedom that will last.

One of the sad things about the past few years in America has been the passivity of majority opinion in the face of racist terrorism and discrimination against minorities. Whatever the cause of this passivity, the corrosion of the democratic conscience means the removal of the strongest rivet from our tradition of civil liberties. The sense of society is basic to all freedom, and to the willingness to fight for it.

We talk of racist threats as threats to minorities. They are that. But in a deeper sense they are threats to the majorities themselves. I shall breathe more freely for the future of America when I see the democratic conscience of America rising to the defense not of the minorities, but of the common stakes that minorities and majorities alike have in human decency and the expansion of man's spirit.

FREEDOM OF SPEECH
AND THE PRESS

BY JAMES LAWRENCE FLY

Former Chairman of the
Federal Communications Commission

WITH ALL OUR TOMES and columns on free speech we nevertheless have an impressively consistent record of unenlightened treatment. On few subjects have we been so articulate; on hardly any subject have our words been so inadequate. Legal research and expression have moved along the narrow channel of legislative and case history. But where have we achieved the heights affording a comprehensive view of the forces impinging on speech and the press?

I shall endeavor here to stress the need for definition and to mention a few of the markers along the broad boundaries, hoping thereby to demonstrate the breadth and complexity of the problem—and the crying need for intelligent delineation and analysis.

At the outset we should endeavor to ascertain the basic purpose of free speech. Counsel for the press has said that the substance of the basic freedom of free speech is merely the absence of governmental restraint. Others have contended that the real purpose of free speech is the clothing of the individual with the legal power of expression as an end in itself. The individual citizen is thus enabled to talk himself out—"to blow off steam," as it were—and thereby to achieve some degree of mental catharsis.

These views are related and are now of considerable currency. But both are fallacies. If either of these views represents our ultimate goal, we may as well immediately abandon all hope of progress. Neither view is capable of advancing the public welfare, for neither shows awareness of the significant purpose of freedom. Both history and logic compel us to accept a different point of view.

It was early recognized that democracy rests upon the capacity of the people intelligently to govern themselves. In the outset free speech and a free press were accepted as the best means for the diffusion to the public of the ideas and the information necessary for intelligent self-government. Fully aware of the facts, the people could be expected to judge contending points of view wisely. It was this knowledge which prompted Jefferson frequently to stress the great need for an informed public opinion. "Were it left to me," he once wrote, "to decide whether we should have a government without newspapers, or newspapers without a government, I should not hesitate a moment to prefer the latter." Washington also knew that democracy rested on a freely and fully informed electorate, for he too uttered a strong demand for the broad diffusion of information to the public.

It was thus recognized that if this freedom was to

mean anything in our democracy, it must serve the needs of the people. Yet today millions read or listen while only one man transmits his ideas. Democracy's stake is at the receiving end more than ever before. Walt Whitman once said: "I say there can be no safety for these states without free tongues and ears willing to hear the tongues." What happens to the speaking tongues and, especially, to the listening ears is what must concern us now. "Safety for these states" is involved, and clearly we are concerned with the ears and the eyes. In the light of this great interest, what is freedom of speech? What do the people of a democracy require?

A few objectives are readily obvious: (1) free access to all pertinent news sources; (2) ways and means for the ready and adequate collection and distribution of news; (3) full presentation of fact and opinion; (4) presentation of opposing points of view and argument; (5) the absence of bias, prejudice, suppression, or distortion; (6) the absence of bottlenecks, overconcentration of control, or domination by a few special interests, especially where the pipe lines to the market place of thought are limited in number; (7) the presence of diversity in the control of news sources and of mechanisms for news distribution to the public.

In other words, we must cling to the theory that ideas, good and bad, must have access to the market place of thought, clashing in open competition in the bid for popular acceptance. Mr. Justice Holmes of the Supreme Court of the United States has said:

When men have realized that time has upset many fighting faiths, they may come to believe even more than they believe the very foundations of their own conduct that the ultimate good desired is better reached by free trade in ideas—that the best test of truth is the power of the thought to get itself accepted in the competition of the market, and that truth is the only ground upon which their wishes safely can be carried out.

With Mr. Justice Holmes and his colleague, Mr. Justice Brandeis, the Darwinian theory of the survival of the fittest was in effect carried over from the field of biology into the realm of opinion. Theirs was the fervent belief that as long as men were free to pour their ideas into the market place, and other men were free to choose among them, the ideas entitled to survival would survive. They looked for more than a mental catharsis or an impotent government.

Competition in the field of commodities has always been recognized as the fundamental principle of our economic system. Competition in the field of ideas is even more basic to our democratic way of life. Unless particular ideas are pitted against others or, at the very least, unless the opportunity exists for such encounter, there can be no freedom of thought worth anything.

Three hundred years before Holmes, Milton said:

And though all the winds of doctrine were let loose to play upon the earth, so Truth be in the field, we do ingloriously, by licensing and prohibiting, to misdoubt her strength. Let her and falsehood grapple; whoever knew Truth put to the worse in a free and open encounter?

Now Milton may have been a bit optimistic in his statistics; I own that truth may lose an occasional battle.

But I submit that here is the system to which a democracy must pin its faith. Jefferson, always publicly true to his faith in this grand experiment in freedom, came privately to despair of its operation. As to the possible existence of a newspaper restrained to "true facts" and "sound principles," he said: "I fear such a paper would find few subscribers." Late in life he thought that "the man who never looks into a newspaper is better informed than he who reads them." Recently I have come to have a sympathetic understanding of Jefferson's despondency, but that understanding has only emphasized the great need for the protection of the principle and for such an insight into the problem as will ensure the public interest. It is here that we must begin a realistic appraisal.

All of us are familiar with the legalistic problem raised by governmental restraints on speech. Legislative action is quickly and publicly stricken down: Joe Doaks, arrested in the town square, goes to the Supreme Court and is vindicated. Neither the federal government nor the state is permitted to interfere. This is well and good. But does that ensure to the public in a modern complex society the benefits of free speech? Of course not. The restraints on competition in the market place of thought are both grave and numerous. The oft-repeated axiom that liberty is never truly won but must be fought for anew each age is just another way of saying that each age brings forth its own threat to freedom—a threat which arises out of and is dictated by the very characteristics of the age. As soon as the repressive influence of one era dissipates itself or is beaten down, the next one produces its own like force, a force which is new in character and against which the liberalizing weapons of the previous era are useless.

We live in an age of machines, mass production, high-pressure merchandizing, monopolies, and near monopolies. The present-day threat—the increasing domination of the media of communication by a few economic entities, and the resultant lessening of opportunities for the full, free spread of all kinds and shades of opinion—is the begotten child of technology and big business. It is this threat which must be understood.

Guarantees of freedom do not operate *in vacuo;* they take on substance only in the light of the setting in which they are applied. None of us today can have direct knowledge of the issues that vitally affect us. Town meetings are things of the past. The public rostrum no longer plays the role it once did. Because of the evolution of modern means of transportation and communication, the world has shrunk, and the emphasis has shifted from local to national and international problems. At the same time, all other channels of communication have paled into insignificance beside the three mighty pipe lines which today hourly feed into the market place of thought the fare that nourishes the minds of millions: the newspapers, the movies, and the radio.

The industrial revolution produced not only the press, the movies, and the radio, but also huge combinations of capital and power over these three media. These combinations are the large newspaper chains, the press associations, the syndicates, the magazine giants, the Hollywood "majors," and the big broadcasting chains. The actual wielders of power are the guiding geniuses of these entities, no more than a score or two of men.

We may assume, for our purposes here, that they are as wise and fair as could be selected by any method. We are concerned only with the need for diversity of control over the various media so that the public may have access to a variety of opinions. The fact is that the entities whose destinies these men guide have cut down diversity to a perilous degree. And the sheer problem of achieving diversity—and of avoiding an overconcentration of the controls of the pipe lines of communication—is itself of gravest importance.

Since 1900 the population has increased from 76 to 135 million, while the number of newspapers has declined from 2350 dailies to 1850. Many of the best of these have been absorbed by national chains, and regional chains have tended toward domination of large local areas. Magazine and newspaper empires have moved out to encompass radio stations, network programs, and even some network interest. A third of the radio stations are owned by the varied press interests. Most of these are closely affiliated with the national networks. The networks did control—and may yet seek to control—all the most valuable time on the hundreds of stations affiliated with them. News from the big press associations is channeled through the network newsrooms and thence out to all the stations on the "net." The "nets" themselves have some news sources, and both stories of fact and opinion originate in that news service. The nation's most powerful advertisers sponsor news programs and frequently select their own commentators. Until recently, single owners in a number of cases controlled two radio stations in a single city—sometimes the only stations. In some instances chain newspapers dominated both press and radio in a single city.

As a result of this trend, one of the very real problems is the ever-shrinking market place of thought. Hence we need to remember that a free press can best be safeguarded, and democracy thereby most faithfully served, by *diversity*.

Bias is less damaging when the people have a free choice of ideas. And diversity in the output is a better safeguard than the vain hope for unbiased reporting—however great the ideal of unbiased reporting. For, after all, all news and all opinion originate with people. And people, of course, don't see alike. A writer chooses his words with the same personal choice and skill—to achieve his desired effect—that the artist uses in painting a scene. Molded by a long train of experience and of thought, the writer's personality colors every description of nearly every factual situation, regardless of the most desperate efforts to be purely objective. Any opinion presents an a fortiori case. Diversity is therefore the greatest alleviating force, the best reducer of opinion to fact.

It may well be urged that the concentration of control over the pipe lines of thought is not an evil so long as the control is beneficent; and it is true that a slight

amount of diversity can be achieved by a grant of freedom to editors, writers, news reporters, and commentators. But this freedom has not been granted! And even
if it were, I doubt that we can ever afford to rely upon
the beneficent exercise of extremely great power. Democracy cannot rest on so slender a reed, for the relation of great economic power to communications of
any type tends inevitably to exercise some degree of
influence, no matter how slight, over news and opinion.
The comic strips, for example, might, offhandedly, be
considered one of the most innocuous forms of occupying readers' minds—if they ever have anything to do
with minds. But even the comics manage to exercise a
real degree of influence. Some of them have enough
effect to warrant their being described as reactionary or
progressive. It is reported, for example, that the President thanked one comic strip artist for his aid on lease-
lend. Other examples, equally unexpected, might be
cited, but a few of the ramifications of the problem of
free speech are now, I hope, clear enough.

Some facets of radio broadcasting will make more
clear the implications of our general discussion.

In the field of broadcasting the Communications
Commission has taken several steps to alleviate con-
centrations of control and restraints on the speech
mechanisms and, affirmatively, to increase those mechanisms.

First, we grappled with the problem of the domination by a couple of national networks of the many radio
stations throughout the country. After a thorough investigation, including lengthy public hearings, the

Commission issued its so-called "Antimonopoly" Regulations. These were important because they dealt with a serious overconcentration of control over the pipe lines of speech to most of the areas in the country.

One of the major benefits accomplished by those regulations was the separation of the Red and the Blue Networks. We have, and have had for a decade, four, and only four, national networks. The Radio Corporation of America owned and operated two of them, the Red and the Blue. In view of the limited number of these important, nation-wide, free speech mechanisms, I need not emphasize the rationale behind the policy of requiring their separation.

Other regulations were adopted consistent with the same general policy of limiting concentration and of achieving diversity of control over radio. We found that the networks by contract controlled all of the desirable time on their various affiliated stations throughout the country, thus dominating the choice of programs and otherwise exercising too large a measure of control over the many local radio stations. The regulations relaxed those particular restraints so that local stations now retain control over the programs they put on the air, including those broadcast during the popular hours of the evening. This enables them to put on programs of their own choice, to get programs from any source they choose, and to reject any network program which is deemed unsatisfactory. The national networks are made up of stations owned by the network in several important cities and of affiliated, but independently owned, stations in other cities. Again, in order to ensure as much diversity as possible, particularly in those places where radio facilities are limited, it was provided in the regulations that the networks might not retain ownership of a station in any city where there were only a few stations—in other words, where there was not adequate competition.

It is now a matter of history, though it is indicative of a great deal of the history in this entire field, that the networks opposed those regulations with two arguments. One was that the regulations would bring about economic ruination. This has already been answered. The networks are making more money now than they ever did. The other was that restoring to the many stations throughout the country greater control over their own time, the power to accept or reject programs, and the power to exercise their responsibilities as licensees was an infringement of free speech. Resort to the institutional guaranty of free speech in order to thwart a progressive step is not novel, but here, where the very regulations being attacked were designed to promote free speech, the application of the technique was at least unusual. The argument could not, and did not, stand analysis.

The problem of overconcentration of control on a national basis, with which the Antimonopoly Regulations were concerned, had its counterpart in the local broadcasting field.

The Commission has taken a number of other steps to the same end of diversifying control over radio facilities. The overconcentration of control in a local community presented by the ownership by single interests of more than one station in the same city was dealt with recently by requiring separate ownership and control of the stations. Incidentally, that measure is progressing satisfactorily, as all of these measures have progressed, without economic injury to a single party concerned. The Commission also made an extensive investigation of the problem presented by the joint ownership of broadcasting stations and newspapers serving the same community. In a policy announced last year, the Commission noted "the importance of avoiding monopoly of the avenues of communicating fact and opinion to the public" and unanimously agreed to the general principle that "diversification of control of such media is desirable." Instead of adopting a general rule in this field, however, the Commission concluded to apply the necessary "public interest" considerations in the processing of individual applications.

There is also, perhaps, in the offing a further policy which will limit the total number of standard broadcast stations under any one ownership, no matter where located. This policy has already been adopted for television and frequency modulation broadcasting. In television we have provided that no single owner may control more than five stations. There is a similar provision in the frequency modulation field. These new broadcasting services will be powerful instruments of speech and persuasion. In television particularly, where sight and audio reception are combined, the broadcaster will have very great power over people's thoughts and necessarily over public opinion.

Under the Communications Act the Commission is,

of course, expressly forbidden any power of censorship. It cannot require a station either to accept or to reject a program. But free speech is a duty as much as it is a right, and broadcasting is a responsibility as well as a privilege. And by decision and policy the Commission has sought to obtain, and I believe has succeeded in obtaining, acceptance of the principle that the broadcaster holds control of these powerful free speech mechanisms in trust for the people.

Bear in mind there is one man at the transmitter, one man free to speak; but there are millions who are listening—the very people freedom of speech is designed to protect. Their interests are paramount. The station owner has a monopoly or quasi monopoly over a wave length, but that wave length is licensed for use only in the *public interest*. If you conceive of free speech as a right of the listener, then you cannot take the position that the operator of the broadcasting station can do whatever he chooses with the powerful instrument he has been licensed to use. It must be remembered that for the first time radio has made free speech a practical, a living, reality outside of the local town hall and public square. With the emphasis today upon national and international issues, no person standing in the town square can hope to have any substantial effect upon public opinion. Over the radio, particularly over a network, he can. Radio is a powerful organ—doubtless the most powerful that has ever existed in the entire field of speech and the press.

A very important principle inheres in this view of broadcasting. There must be full and fair presentation of facts; reporting must be balanced and not biased. A station operator cannot devote his station to the support of his own pet policies; he must afford an adequate presentation of the various sides of controversial issues. It is important that parties have access to the air upon a nondiscriminatory basis. Until recently a concern with a cathartic to sell could get on the air to hawk it, but a labor union or a philosophical society could not buy time.

Although, as I have said, the Commission has no power of censorship and thus can in no way dictate what programs shall or shall not be broadcast, it does periodically review, as it is required by the Communications Act to do, the over-all operations of a station. And in connection with the consideration of applications for renewal of license, it can and does apply the test of whether or not there has been a well-balanced program service, whether or not there has been a fair and full, rather than a one-sided, presentation of controversial matters, and whether or not time has been made available on a nondiscriminatory basis to various groups of people and types of organizations. During the past few years, those principles have been increasingly accepted by the industry itself, and I believe that as a result radio—and this will be especially true of the newer frequency modulation and television broadcasting—will more nearly realize its potentialities as a great instrument for free speech.

In the field of international communications we have sought to lay the groundwork for the establishment of the universal principle of the freedom to listen. It is idle to talk about a free press in the world of tomorrow so long as there is any impediment in the collection, transmission, or distribution of news by American companies throughout the world. Kent Cooper has written an excellent book, *Barriers Down,* in which he describes the generation-long struggle of the Associated Press: first, in its effort to live with the foreign monopolies dominating the flow of world news; finally, its success in beating down the barriers of exclusion and discrimination. But many barriers still remain. It must be clear that there is no free press adequate to the needs of the American public when large portions of the world are only darkly reported to us. And we have suffered greatly from having news about our country go abroad only as edited by the news monopoly of some foreign country. Little wonder that abroad we were considered a nation of idle rich, of movie stars, and of gang rule. In our own interest our press deserves the strong support of this nation in the effort to communicate freely with all other nations and news sources and to distribute freely American news of America.

Moreover, there can be no free press, in the full sense, so long as our communications are burdened by onerous rates—imposed by foreign monopolies—and pointedly discriminatory against us.

This nation must cease channeling its communications through a third country, as we now do in some important instances; we must establish a comprehensive, unified system of instantaneous communication with all important points on the globe. We must tolerate no unfair discrimination or impediment.

Do you remember how Woodrow Wilson described the "radio revolution"? Although radio was still in its infancy then—this was September, 1919—President Wilson prophetically foresaw its immense global potentialities. He said:

Do you not know that the world is all now one single whispering gallery? Those antennae of the wireless telegraph are the symbols of our age. All the impulses of mankind are thrown out upon the air and reach to the ends of the earth.

What Wilson foresaw is coming to pass in greater measure. And its coming demands our preparing for it.

Yet onerous restraints on listening can be found in one part of the world or another now under Axis domination. For example, consider the practices in Germany. The state controls the manufacture of radio receivers so that it is impossible to obtain a set capable of receiving a short-wave signal. Furthermore, the standard broadcast range is limited to the German propaganda centers. Not willing to give the German people even a sporting chance to sneak a listen to the ideas of the world, Goebbels makes doubly certain only approved broadcasts are heard by jamming any *verboten* utterances as they occur.

But the will to listen dies hard, and the mechanical precautions have had to be strengthened with legal sanctions. An inhuman German statute provides the death penalty for persistent "black listening." Those people guilty of one act of "black listening" are merely thrown into a concentration camp. A wife with guilty knowledge of her husband's "black listening" goes to

76

the concentration camp too. The Japanese militarists go a step further than their German colleagues; they kill and torture Japanese people for what they call "dangerous thoughts." Such fear and tyranny stagger our imagination. We can hardly imagine that we could be taking our lives in our hands by merely *thinking* of turning on our radios.

Such moral darkness is a breeding ground for suspicion. There can be no understanding when people are shrouded by the ideas only of the Fuehrer, no matter who he may be. The end product for these benighted people is a pathological conviction that war against their fellow man is a noble thing.

It would be harmful beyond prediction to have world radio restricted, either by hiding behind a restrictive world policy or by allowing any individual nation to frustrate a fine policy by adopting restrictions of a mechanical nature. I cannot but feel that the future peace and security of the people of the world must rest in large measure upon enlightenment. If we are to have an enlightened world, we can attain it only by following enlightened principles. The thoughts of men must be expressed freely and openly; otherwise, thinking dries up. Any substitute for thought which is rushed into the vacuum of ignorance is bound to be dangerous. Witness what we are fighting today.

Let me remind you that freedom to listen encompasses more than the ability to spin the dial without fear. With only the general policy I have discussed as a safeguard, the transmitters of all nations must individually foster a free and complete exchange of thought and the optimum diffusion of knowledge. The right to hear new ideas is part of the freedom to listen and is as much the burden of my theme as is the inadequacy of free speech in the absence of effective mechanisms and of ears able to listen. Universally accepted must be the freedom of all peoples to listen without fear and without restraint.

This has been a long excursion, yet I have barely touched upon the major problems. In a democracy so much depends upon a really free speech and press that I hope we all can come to know more of the problem. *Let us move.* Let us get the issues into the open, discuss them freely, and endeavor to bring the force of public opinion to bear on the various mechanisms affecting them. Few undertakings could be more worth while.

CIVIL LIBERTY AND
PUBLIC OPINION

BY ROBERT E. CUSHMAN

*Goldwin Smith Professor of Government,
Cornell University*

THE TERM "civil liberty" was not in the common vocabulary of the Founding Fathers. They spoke rather of the "rights of man," or "natural rights," or "inalienable rights," or in some cases "the rights of Englishmen," thus using the terminology of the eighteenth-century French philosophers or the English Whigs—or both. They were pinning labels, however, on rights and freedoms which seemed to them very real because they had been won by long struggle and bitter sacrifice, and these they listed fully and precisely in our constitutional bills of rights. We no longer speak about the "rights of man" or "natural rights"; we use the term civil liberty, but we mean by it these same rights and freedoms which our forefathers won for us and embodied in our bills of rights, and which are, therefore, under the protection of our courts of law.

Nor do we find the term "public opinion" in current use among the men who founded our government. Political democracy was not very far advanced at that time and any "public" which was likely to have any articulate "opinion" was rather sure to be fairly small. These men, however, had won their independence from Great Britain by a war which was begun and carried through by the force of what we should now call public opinion. They justified and rationalized this revolutionary enterprise in Jefferson's statement in the Declaration of Independence that "governments are instituted among men, deriving their just powers from the consent of the governed." In making sure that in the new government of an independent America the "consent of the governed" should be the basis of power, they adopted the principle of majority rule, though as Professor Becker pointed out in the opening lecture, they surrounded the actual operation of majority rule with a good many checks and balances. But majority rule in a democracy clearly implies, in fact requires, the existence of what we should call public opinion, or perhaps numerous public opinions, in order to determine who are the majority and how they wish to rule. Our forefathers were familiar with many of the facts of public opinion even if they did not use that name.

In the large and growing literature dealing with the subject, it is not easy to find a simple and adequate definition of public opinion. A hundred and twenty-five years ago the British statesman, Sir Robert Peel, in a letter to a friend referred sourly to "that great compound of folly, weakness, prejudice, wrong feeling, right feeling, obstinacy and newspaper paragraphs, which is called public opinion." A competent modern scholar, writing in the *Encyclopedia of the Social Sciences*, tells us that:

82

Public opinion . . . is a deeply pervasive organic force, intimately bound up with the ideological and emotional interplay of the social groupings in which since the earliest times gregarious individuals have come together; it articulates and formulates not only the deliberative judgments of the rational elements within the collectivity, but the evanescent common will, which somehow integrates and momentarily crystallizes the sporadic sentiments and loyalties of the masses of the population.

This is all perfectly true, no doubt, but it is not very useful for the purposes of our present informal discussion. I shall not attempt to compete with this definition but shall content myself with saying that in a constitutional democracy like ours, which is based on the will of the people, and in which the officers of government are the servants of the people, the people, in groups of varying size and shifting complexion, regularly or at unexpected intervals and in many different ways manage to make their will known. This is public opinion. It may for the moment be quiescent; it may seem to you or to me to be ignorant or biased. But it is the motive power on which democracy runs. As James Bryce put it:

Towering over Presidents and state governors, over Congress and state legislatures, over conventions and the vast machinery of party, public opinion stands out, in the United States, as the master of servants who tremble before it.

Civil liberty and public opinion are the two foundation stones upon which constitutional democracy rests. Both are indispensable to the existence of constitutional democracy; and each is indispensable to the existence of the other. The men who established our government were well aware of the relationship between civil liberty and public opinion, although they called them by different names. They had earned their civil liberties the hard way. They had bargained for them and fought for them, and they had suffered the humiliation which comes with the denial of civil liberty by an external sovereign authority. When a successful revolution replaced the sovereignty of the British Crown by the sovereignty of the American people, the Founding Fathers were shrewd enough to know that this change did not automatically safeguard civil liberty. If ultimate governmental power rested now in the will of the people, as measured by majority rule, the fact must be faced that majorities may be as unjust and brutal as a despotic monarch. Civil liberties could be made safe only if placed beyond the reach of temporary majorities by being firmly embedded in carefully drawn bills of rights. Thus these early statesmen established the machinery for the exercise of organized popular self-control and set up safeguards against their own folly and intolerance. With the alertness of men scarred by experience, wary of the unknown dangers of democracy, these men saw clearly the crucially important relationship between public opinion and civil liberty.

We have had a hundred and fifty years of experience in this country both with civil liberty and with public opinion. We have learned many things about public opinion which our forefathers could not know. But I am afraid we have forgotten some of the things about civil liberty which were indelibly impressed on the minds of men who had fought to achieve it. And one of the things we find easy to forget is that neither civil liberty nor public opinion can exist in a democratic state without the other. It is this interdependence of civil liberty and public opinion, together with the challenge and the warning which it presents, which I wish to discuss. What I have to say may be stated in the form of four propositions, each of which I shall attempt to establish. They are as follows: First, public opinion can exist only where and when civil liberty is kept alive. Second, civil liberty will exist only so long as it is supported and defended by public opinion. Third, public opinion with respect to civil liberty today shows dangerous signs of being confused, timid, and complacent. Fourth, courageous leadership and sound education are vitally necessary if we are to keep alive a public opinion which values civil liberty and will demand its effective protection.

No thoughtful person will reject my first proposition, that public opinion, in any meaningful sense, cannot exist unless civil liberty is zealously protected. The very term "public opinion" makes sense only when applied to a community of free men. We Americans pride ourselves upon being free. We are free from arbitrary arrest and ruthless and unjust criminal procedure. We are free from the confiscation of our property. We are free to worship, to think, to speak, to print, and to assemble together. Any citizen who is capable of forming an opinion upon any subject is entirely free to do so. If he needs facts to aid him, he will find more at his elbow than he can use. If the subject of his interest is controversial, he will find arguments and evidence on both sides. If he wishes to form as fair and judicial an opinion as possible, he is quite free to read or listen to both sides. If, on the other hand, he does not wish to run the risk of being converted from a preconceived position, he is equally free to read or listen only to those who agree with him and strengthen his original opinions. More important still, he is not forbidden to read or listen to those who support the opinions of his choice merely because they are the opinions of an unorthodox minority. Not only may he thus form his opinions freely, but he may express them freely. He will not be arrested and sent to a concentration camp for so doing. He can express them orally if others are willing to listen to him, which, however, under no circumstances are they obliged to do. If he feels strongly enough about his opinions, he can hire a hall and expound them from the platform. If he has equally zealous opponents, he may either debate with them publicly, or he may decline to do so, as his preference dictates. If he is reasonably literate, he can probably find some one of the twelve thousand odd daily or weekly newspapers in the country willing to print a statement of his views, or to allow him to protest in print against the previously stated views of his opponents. In short, in this atmosphere of freedom, you and I —just ordinary citizens—not only enjoy the satisfaction to be derived from self-expression, but we may freely contribute our influence to the formation of that powerful force, public opinion.

It is natural for the individual citizen to think about civil liberty in terms of its effect upon him or upon someone else whose rights have been threatened or denied. But we must not ignore the vastly important stake which the community and the nation have in the safeguarding of these liberties. The free public dissemination of ideas and opinions by free speech and a free press is the very bloodstream of a democratic government based upon the will of the people. How can there be a "will of the people," or how can we possibly hope to know what it is, without the full public discussion of issues of public policy? Only by the open clash of opinion, by the matching of arguments and the comparing of evidence, can the people enjoy a fair opportunity to form an intelligent and reasoned judgment. You and I as individuals can coddle ourselves if we wish by reading or listening only to people with whom we agree. We are not required to read *PM* or the *Chicago Tribune* if we do not wish to do so. But a democratic community, if it is to remain democratic, cannot black out the opinions which the majority dislike or fear. It must always keep open the opportunity of a minority to become a majority by means of peaceful persuasion. One of the virtues of our party system in American politics is that there is always a minority party and sometimes several. Nothing more calamitous can befall a political party than to grow so powerful that vigorous opposition and public criticism weaken or die out. Politicians and statesmen recognize and act upon this principle, as is shown by the position of dignity and influence accorded the minority leaders in our Senate and House of Representatives. The British go even further than we do in this respect. The leader of the minority in the House of Commons goes by the resounding title of

Leader of His Majesty's Opposition, and he receives a special salary in payment of the services he renders in this capacity. In this way the two most important legislative bodies in the world assure themselves of the advantages of full, frank, and fearless presentation of divergent points of view on questions of major policy in an effort to inform their judgments. The people of the nation at large, however, must rely for this vitally important service upon freedom of speech and a free press, and it is of the most urgent importance that every shade of opinion be openly and fully expressed. Perhaps each one of us here could name certain newspapers, columnists, or radio commentators that are our particular abominations. As a thoughtful citizen, however, each of us ought to say to himself, "How glad I am that I live in a country in which these ignorant, prejudiced, pigheaded demagogues can say and print these outrageous things, because as long as they can do so, I know that the civil liberties are still alive upon which a democratic government based upon public opinion must depend."

Probably the most tragically conclusive evidence to prove that public opinion cannot exist without civil liberty is to be seen in the fate of German democracy. There is nothing in Germany which can be called public opinion, save as it hides in cellars or is confined in concentration camps. There is no such thing as civil liberty in Germany. As a political force the "people of Germany," in distinction from their Nazi oppressors, died long ago of the pernicious anemia induced by the complete obliteration of the civil liberties of the German people.

My second proposition is that civil liberty can survive only so long as it is supported and defended by public opinion. I do not mean that we shall lose our liberties every time public opinion becomes intolerant and popular hysteria results in some invasion of minority rights. Majorities sometimes yield to the temptation to override the civil liberties of those who oppose them. As we have seen, our forefathers realized this danger, and that is why civil liberties were firmly embedded in the provisions of our Constitution, and why majority action was hedged about by an elaborate system of checks and balances. They provided for an appeal from Philip drunk to Philip sober, from the public opinion of the moment to the deliberate judgment and conscience of the people. In short, I am not talking about the public opinion of the moment, but the public opinion which is continuing and habitual. If as a people we lose our basic loyalty to the principles of freedom of speech and freedom of the press, if an intrenched majority are able to convince us that their conception of our American way of life must not be publicly opposed or criticized, and that those who discuss changing our political or economic institutions and practices are dangerous and subversive criminals who ought to be locked up, then neither the First Amendment in our Federal Bill of Rights, nor the Supreme Court of the United States will be able to keep alive free speech and a free press. We must never forget that the constitutional guarantees with which we have surrounded our civil liberties are nothing more than restraints which the American people have placed upon themselves, and that those restraints are no stronger than the steady and deliberate will of the American people to be bound by them.

There are a number of reasons why this is so, and plenty of evidence that it is so. It is true in the first place because, in a democratic government, public officers generally speaking will be guided by what they believe is the will of the people. This is especially true of our representatives in state legislatures and in Congress. No Congressman needs to resort to political philosophy to convince himself that his first and last obligation is to discover and act upon the wishes of the voters who put him in office and who, he hopes, will keep him there. In fact, so supersensitive are most of our legislators to what they think is the voice of the people that one of the most serious dangers to civil liberty in this country lies in the triggerlike willingness of some of our legislatures to translate promptly into law the intolerant and sometimes brutal impulses of a temporarily aroused public opinion. Thus we have the notorious West Virginia statute which makes it a crime to advocate or to teach "any ideals hostile to those now or henceforth existing under the constitution and laws of this state." Thus we have the resolution passed unanimously by the city council of Cambridge, Massachusetts, a few years ago forbidding the circulation within the city limits of any literature in which the word Lenin or Leningrad appeared. Fortunately, the mayor of the city vetoed the resolution. Thus we have the recent action of the school board in Passaic, New Jersey, which removed the *Reader's Digest* from school reading rooms because a majority of the board found it to be prejudiced, reactionary, and hostile to labor. This action also was later reversed. These are exaggerated and unusual incidents. But one cannot observe how Congress and our state legislatures over the last twenty-five years have dealt with civil liberty problems without realizing that these legislative bodies will usually enact the repressive measures demanded by a hysterical and short-lived public opinion, and will almost certainly pass the repressive laws demanded by a long-range and deliberate public opinion.

The same thing is true of our executive officers. They too are servants of the people. It is their duty to enforce and administer the laws which are enacted by the legislature. Law enforcement is not an automatic mechanical process. It is a very human process calling for the exercise of wide discretion. A legislature swayed by a gust of hysterical public opinion may pass a law broadly repressive of free speech and press, like the West Virginia statute just mentioned. But it is the prosecutor, the district attorney, or the attorney general, who decides whether A, B, and C shall be arrested, indicted, and brought to trial for violating that statute. These executive officers may act with ruthless and efficient zeal to suppress minority opinion by a campaign of witch-hunting, or they may proceed with an even-tempered caution to enforce the law only in cases of its clear and flagrant violation. We have had many examples of prosecuting officers who have courageously withstood the demands of popular clamor for the suppression of civil liberty. In his notable book, *Free Speech in the United States,* which should be required reading for every citizen, Professor Chafee tells us that during the last war in the Boston area "we had in our midst a large foreign-born population, much of it unfriendly, by race at least, to the allied cause, much of it possessing radical views. The United States District Attorney in Massachusetts, George W. Anderson, refused to institute a single prosecution although much was said and written which would have been punished elsewhere. No record exists of a single bomb explosion, act of sabotage, or evasion of the draft, or desertion, which may be traced to such an unpunished utterance. There is not one bit of evidence that the cause of the war suffered in Massachusetts because this district attorney disregarded clamor and adhered to liberal principles." During the present war the Department of Justice in Washington has exercised a similar cool-headed restraint. In contrast to thousands of prosecutions during the last war, the Department, with much tougher laws on the statute books, has prosecuted only about one hundred persons for sedition or other "morale-impairing" crimes. We must bear in mind, however, that there has been no strong public opinion during the present war which has demanded the suppression of minority opinion, chiefly because, as Mr. Lerner pointed out, there is no important and articulate minority opinion which opposes the war and which, therefore, anyone cares to suppress. On the other hand, during the last war public opinion in large areas of the country did demand witch-hunting on a wide scale, with the result that state and federal prosecuting officers gave the people what they demanded and we had witch-hunting.

It may be suggested, however, that civil liberty will survive in this country even if public opinion no longer supports it because our courts will protect the civil liberties guaranteed by our bills of rights no matter if a strong public opinion clamors for their sacrifice and only a feeble public opinion rallies to their support. Fortunately, our experience entitles us to place great confidence in our courts as the defenders of civil liberty. They have often done in the past, and they continue to do, a splendid job in this respect. But it would be tragic for us to fail to realize how inadequate are our courts of law to keep civil liberty alive in this country if the people themselves abandon that responsibility. In the first place, we must bear in mind that in many cases a court cannot prevent the suppression of a man's civil liberty; it can only give him some kind of relief or redress after his unhappy experience is over and, frequently, a long time after it is over. None of the cases during the first World War in which suppression by the government of free speech and press was alleged reached the Supreme Court for review until from six months to a year after the armistice. If the police wantonly break up an orderly public meeting, as they used to do in Jersey City, it is not of much practical help to be told by the Supreme Court two years later that the police action was an unlawful invasion of the constitutional right of freedom of assembly. In the second place, the courts can protect civil liberty as a rule only when some person with energy, courage, and money enough fights for his rights by bringing a case into court. A clear example of this is found in the situation with respect to the so-called "third degree." The Supreme Court of the United States has repeatedly and vigorously denounced the third degree as a violation of a constitutionally protected civil liberty and has set aside convictions resting upon evidence secured by police brutality. Everyone knows, however, that third degree methods are still in common use in spite of their illegality, since the average police officer gambles upon the knowledge that only one arrested person in a hundred will have either the means or the courage to assert his rights in court. It is clear, in short, that judicial protection to civil liberty in its very nature operates only at the perimeter of the area within which the threats to civil liberties arise.

We must face the further fact that the courts themselves are manned by judges who are themselves people, and who are not immune to the influences which shape the thinking of their fellow citizens. They cannot be expected to balk or defy a powerful public opinion firmly established and of long duration. We have had some disturbing examples of courts and judges yielding to the volatile public opinion of the moment. It will be remembered that federal judges construed and enforced the notorious Sedition Act of 1798 with cynical brutality. Toward the close of the first World War and after the collapse of Russia, American soldiers were sent to Murmansk and Vladivostok on an expedition which Newton D. Baker, the Secretary of War, later described as "nonsense from the beginning." But in the summer of 1918 a group of young Russians circulated in New York some literature sharply attacking the government for this ill-considered expedition. They were convicted of sedition and sentenced to prison for twenty years, and the Supreme Court of the United States in the Abrams case upheld their conviction and declared that it involved no violation of freedom of speech or press. These are perhaps exceptional instances of judicial surrender to the public opinion of the moment, and over against them should be placed a long list of cases in which the Supreme Court, especially during and since the courageous leadership of Mr. Chief Justice Hughes, has strengthened the judicial bulwarks surrounding our civil liberties by holding unconstitutional laws suppressing or abridging them. But if the cause of civil liberty in this country ceases to command the loyalty and support of deliberate and thoughtful public opinion, I see no reason to suppose that our courts will be able or willing to carry on the defense of civil liberty alone. Judges are not going to be able to keep civil liberty alive in a nation that no longer values it.

Perhaps the most persuasive evidence in support of the point I am making, that civil liberty cannot exist without the support of public opinion, is to be found in the experience of the South in dealing with the civil liberties of the Negro. The Fourteenth and Fifteenth Amendments to our Constitution undertook to give to the Negro full equality before the law with respect to his civil and political rights. Public opinion in the South has steadily resisted this principle of racial equality before the law and has clung to the doctrine of "white supremacy." The result is that the Negro in the South does not enjoy full equality before the law. Southern legislatures, executive officials, and even judges have been more loyal to Southern public opinion than to the Constitution. And the cause of Negro civil and political liberty is not likely to make much headway in the South as long as that hostile public opinion prevails.

I have been trying to make clear that public opinion in the best sense cannot exist without civil liberty, and that civil liberty cannot survive without the support of public opinion. If this is true, then the vital importance of an intelligent and vigorous public opinion which believes in civil liberty and will not tolerate its suppression stands out sharply. This leads me to my third proposition, that American public opinion with respect to civil liberty falls far short of being sound and vigorous, but shows disturbing signs of being timid, confused, and complacent. Let me explain why I believe this is so.

In the first place, it is perhaps natural for most of us to associate the term "civil liberty" with unpleasant people or events. We are likely to think of it in connection with someone who is about to be arrested, or who is already in prison, and who asserts that his civil liberties have been invaded. Usually he is a member of some minority group since the civil liberties of minorities are, of course, particularly vulnerable. It is very easy for us to look askance at these people. Who are they? They are the Communists, the radicals, the aliens, the crackpots, the agitators, the "lunatic fringe"—in short, those who are always making trouble and getting into trouble. Very few of them are people with whom we care to associate. They are not part of the established and respectable elements in the community. And yet these are the people who usually flash into our minds when the term "civil liberty" is mentioned. Furthermore, most of the literature dealing with the problems of civil liberty is the literature of protest and appeal, put forth either by those who claim that their civil liberties have been violated, or by the crusading organizations or journals which devote themselves to the protection of minority rights. It is likely to be somewhat lurid and impassioned literature, and to plead the causes of unorthodox and sometimes rather disagreeable people. It becomes easy, therefore, to regard those who lecture us about the importance of the Bill of Rights, and exhort us to defend civil liberties, with the same suspicion and distaste with which we regard those queer and annoying people whose civil liberties seem always to need defending. This point of view was amusingly emphasized here on the Cornell campus a few years ago. Some of you will remember the article published in a student magazine in the spring of 1940 entitled, "Reds at Cornell," and written by Mrs. Elizabeth Dilling, the author of *The Red Network*. Mrs. Dilling undertook to leave unexposed no skeletons in Cornell's closet. President Day's previous association with the Rockefeller Foundation, which "for years has subsidized radicalism," clearly makes him a dangerous Red, and on similarly convincing evidence Mrs. Dilling was able to accuse a goodly proportion of the Cornell staff of Communistic leanings and activities. Professor Becker and myself were guilty on several counts, but the one which is pertinent to my present analysis was the charge that I had addressed a student group "on that hackneyed Communist subject, the Bill of Rights and civil liberty." We find this amusing. But what is not amusing is this implication, which appears in the thinking of many people much more normal and rational than Mrs. Dilling, that somehow there must be something wrong, something dangerous or subversive about a man who has too keen an interest in the Bill of Rights and civil liberty. He must want to say things that ought not to be said or do things which ought not to be done, or he would not be so concerned about free speech and other constitutional rights. And a great many good citizens have unconsciously come to feel that there is something about civil liberty and the efforts made to protect it that is not quite respectable. They do not wish to associate themselves publicly with the radical and noisy crowd whose civil liberties seem so often to be at issue. They slide into an attitude of timidity, mixed with snobbishness, which leads them to stand aloof and to refrain from throwing in their influence on the side of the rigid protection of civil liberty.

It is only a short step, however, from this attitude of aloofness and distaste to the attitude that civil liberties really ought not to belong to everybody, but only to people who deserve them as a sort of reward for holding sound opinions and behaving with conservative decorum. If we were to ask citizens at random if they believed in free speech and a free press only for people with whose ideas they agree, most of them would indignantly deny holding any such intolerant view. But it becomes disturbingly evident that a large and growing number of good American citizens do fundamentally believe in free speech only "for our side," even if they would not admit it. Not long ago a student organization at a western university invited Harry Bridges to talk on the problems of organized labor, and he did so. One of the regents of the university, a prosperous businessman, vigorously protested against the holding of such a meeting and declared with engaging candor, "Of course I believe in free speech, but I do not believe in free speech for people like Harry Bridges." This is an attitude of mind which is peculiarly disquieting, because there is no more serious menace to civil liberty than the intolerant man who insists that he is a good liberal.

In any comment on the growth of this attitude of intolerance, this smug assumption that our civil liberties really belong only to the respectable and the orthodox, one cannot ignore the sinister influence of Martin Dies, from 1938 to 1944 chairman of the House Committee to Investigate Un-American Activities. He contributed two ideas to official and unofficial thought and action in the field of civil liberties. These have taken deep root in wide sections of the public opinion of the country, and the result has been an exceedingly dangerous confusion of mind which I regard as a serious threat to American democracy.

Mr. Dies's first and most conspicuous contribution has been to make intolerance synonymous with patriotism. He set out, it is true, to expose genuinely dangerous and subversive people who were an actual menace to the public security. He did expose some, although it now seems clear that our very efficient Federal Bureau of Investigation would have dealt with all of these people quite competently without help from Mr. Dies. He then embarked upon a systematic campaign to suppress freedom of political and economic opinion. This campaign moved under the banner of Americanism; and the approbrious epithet "un-American" was applied to all those who indulged in any open criticism of our existing institutions, our so-called American way of life, or of Mr. Dies. In short, good loyal American citizens who ought to know better were persuaded to give their support to the suppression of free speech and free press on the grotesque theory that they were thereby showing their loyalty to the basic principles of American democracy. Bigotry was made not merely respectable but noble. By the skillful use of labels, or slogans, American public opinion was inoculated with the dangerous idea that true Americanism consists in the stalwart defense of the *status quo* and the suppression of those dangerous and disloyal people who are unpatriotic enough to want to criticize it or suggest any change in it.

Mr. Dies's second contribution to intolerance and to popular confusion of thought with respect to civil liberty took the form of another adroit use of names or labels. Under the guise of attacking Communism he was able to attack all so-called liberal ideas in the field of politics and economics. This was done by pinning the label of Communism on all persons who belonged to any society or organization in which there ever had been any Communist member, or any idea, theory, or action of which any Communist had ever approved. An illustration or two will make this technique clearer. In 1933 thousands of people petitioned President Roosevelt to recognize the Soviet Union, which he did. Professor Becker and I both signed such a petition. So also did nearly all the Communists in the country. This promptly landed Professor Becker and me on Mr. Dies's blacklist of dangerous radicals or at least suspects. The reasoning is quite simple and takes the form of the following syllogism:

Major premise: Communists petitioned for the recognition of Russia.

Minor premise: Becker and Cushman petitioned for the recognition of Russia.

Conclusion: Becker and Cushman are Communists. Mr. Dies did not, of course, invent this process of reasoning. Any student of elementary logic will at once recognize it as the so-called fallacy of an undistributed middle. Mr. Dies merely borrowed it, put the seal of the United States government on it, and used it for eight years to smear as disloyal and subversive such leaders of progressive thought as Henry Wallace, Frank Murphy, Felix Frankfurter, Archibald MacLeish, John Dewey, Bishop Francis J. McConnell, and countless others.

Perhaps the prize example of what might be called the "Dies Committee mind" came to my attention some weeks ago. A federal agent interviewed me in the course of making the customary check on the loyalty of a colleague of mine in a neighboring university, who was being appointed to a confidential post in the government service. This man was not an agent of the Dies Committee but he had apparently learned the Dies method. After the usual routine questions had been asked and answered, the investigator stated that the man in question was a member of Phi Beta Kappa, that a man in New York had told him that there are a lot of Communists and radicals who are members of Phi Beta Kappa, and he wanted my opinion on whether this was in any way prejudicial to my friend. I was entirely unable to convince him that someone had been pulling his leg, and there is no doubt whatever that in this man's mind membership in Phi Beta Kappa is a circumstance so suspicious as to make necessary very careful further investigation of the loyalty of any man who wears the familiar key. The tragedy in all this lies not so much in the danger to free speech and press which comes from the activities of Mr. Dies and men like him, as it does in the fact that so many well-meaning but uncritical people have been swindled by this bad logic into regarding Mr. Dies as the savior of his country and the suppression of minority opinion as a patriotic duty.

I have been tracing what seems to me to be convincing evidence of the growth of an unhealthy public opinion in this country with respect to civil liberty. One cannot, of course, measure with any accuracy just how prevalent the ideas we have been discussing actually are. Certainly they are held by substantial segments of public opinion and are being encouraged by men in positions of responsibility who know better or who ought to know better. Our mistake, insofar as we are making it, has perhaps been a natural one, but it is fundamental and it is very dangerous. We are allowing ourselves to lose sight of the social stake which we have in the maintenance of free speech and a free press and in the effective protection of our other civil liberties. This is a point which Mr. Lerner and Mr. Fly stressed with vigor. Civil liberties must be kept actively alive, not merely in order to protect the individual citizen from brutal and unjust treatment, but in order that American democracy itself may function effectively and that we may have a free government based on the considered will of the people.

My fourth and final point is that if we are to have the sound and discriminating public opinion about our civil liberties which is necessary to the healthy life of constitutional democracy, leadership is needed in the task of developing that public opinion, and in protecting it against the confusion of thought and the fallacies which we have just been describing. Who is to provide that leadership? Where does the responsibility lie for helping the American people to keep firmly and clearly in mind the fundamental value and importance of our civil liberties?

In the first place, major responsibility must be assumed by our public officers in high and low places. Many of these men have duties which involve the management of civil liberties. They have the ear of the people because what they do and what they say is news. From the President down to the chief of police, these officers should seize every opportunity to identify themselves publicly with the principles of free speech and a free press and with the careful safeguarding of the civil liberties of the citizen. Why do we leave the exposition and the defense of our civil liberties to the victims of oppression, to the crackpots, the crusaders, and the agitators, some of whom at least hope to get a chance to abuse the freedoms which we extend to them? By strong and intelligent official utterances on the importance and value of civil liberty we should help counteract in the public mind the impression that civil liberties exist only to protect queer and unpleasant people who are bent on making trouble, and we should emphasize the essential dignity of civil liberty as the cornerstone of American democracy. Let Congress make its position clear by creating a Joint Standing Committee on Civil Liberty. This should be a continuing body so that its policies and activities may be enriched by accumulated experience. It should have an adequate staff, and it should be guaranteed substantial funds. It should have a roving commission to explore the problems relating to civil liberties in both general and specific cases, and to recommend to Congress desirable legislation. It should be a body before which grievances arising out of the supposed abridgments of civil liberties could be fully aired. It should report to Congress on developments in the field of its assignment annually—more frequently if there should be good reason for doing so. If we can afford to spend three quarters of a million dollars on a Committee to Investigate Un-American Activities as defined by Mr. Dies and his colleagues, surely we can afford to spend a reasonable sum on a Committee on American Activities, namely, the sound protection of our constitutional freedoms. It would be very healthy for Congress itself to have such a committee; it would be good for the country to feel that Congress had the wisdom and the courage to take positive action to make its loyalty to civil liberty a matter of record.

In the second place, a heavy responsibility rests upon the members of the American bar not only to aid in individual cases in the legal protection of civil liberties, but to lead public opinion toward a sound and just appraisal of their vast importance. The record of the service rendered to the cause of civil liberties by American lawyers is a very long and honorable one. It stretches all the way from James Otis, defending two Boston merchants against the tyrannical Writs of Assistance in 1761, down to Wendell Willkie, defending the Communist, William Schneiderman, in the Supreme Court in 1943. The American Bar Association and nearly all the state bar associations have special committees on the Bill of Rights or on civil liberties, whose duties are to file briefs as friends of the court in cases in which it appears that the civil liberties of the citizen have been abridged or are threatened. All of this constitutes patriotic service of the highest order. It not only aids the individual defendant whose constitutional rights may have been denied by official action, but it focuses the public mind upon the spectacle of a man like Mr. Willkie vigorously fighting for the legal rights of a Communist labor leader with whose political and economic views he violently disagrees. It emphasizes the common interest which we all have in keeping alive and safeguarding the liberties of every member of the community. For all that the members of the legal profession have done, as individuals or through professional societies, in rendering this public service we should be grateful. But what they have done is only a small part of what they might do. The American lawyer, by virtue of his training, his character, and the nature of his work, stands in the very front rank of the respected and influential leaders of public opinion in the community in which he lives. He cannot escape the obligation to aid by word and deed in the creation and preservation of a public opinion which truly appraises the value and importance of our civil liberties.

This same responsibility rests upon those other professions which are engaged directly and almost exclusively in molding public opinion. No one who has the ear of the public and who makes his living by pouring into that ear facts, opinions, and judgments in an effort to influence popular thinking can fail to realize how dependent he is upon the maintenance of freedom of speech, freedom of the press, and freedom of religion, and how vital those freedoms are to an alert and informed public opinion. Every journalist, every clergyman, every commentator, and every public lecturer in the country should be a loyal and outspoken defender of all the freedoms protected by our bills of rights.

The greatest responsibility of all rests upon our schools, our colleges, and our universities. In the schools of America the citizens of tomorrow enlarge their knowledge, sharpen and cultivate their minds, and acquire a very large part of the code of values by which they will be guided in later life. The men and women who will dominate public opinion in this country a few years hence are now sitting in college and university classrooms all over the country, or will be sitting there when the war is over. What can they get from that experience which will help fit them for posts of leadership in a democracy? I think it is the inescapable duty of the college or university to offer to the leader of tomorrow two things. We must offer him first an intimate knowledge of the history, the principles, the structure, and the actual working of our constitutional democracy. He must know what kind of government it is under which he lives. He must be aware of its weaknesses and its failures, as well as of its achievements and its strength. He must understand clearly the power, actual and potential, of the individual citizen in making democracy work. He must come to know something about public opinion, what it is, where it comes from, and how it behaves. He must see clearly that freedom of speech and freedom of the press and our other civil liberties are not just personal safeguards but are vital parts of the machinery of democratic government. The second thing which a university owes to the leader of tomorrow is to expose him during his years on the campus to an atmosphere of intellectual honesty, of tolerance, of openmindedness, of love for the truth, which is not necessarily learned from textbooks and lectures, but which is the essential life and spirit of a university worthy of the name. Here he may learn to analyse controversial issues, to weigh evidence and arguments, to recognize fallacies—in short, to think clearly and honestly. Our schools, colleges, and universities can render no service of greater value than to produce citizens who are clearheaded and fair-minded. These are the qualities upon which we can hope to build a public opinion which will be aware of the fundamental importance of civil liberty, and which will have the enlightened courage to demand its most generous protection.

Nor can the individual citizen escape responsibility for doing his small share in the cause of civil liberty. He may not be able to make speeches, lead a crusade, or influence official action, and he may easily feel that he is too weak and unimportant to count. But he does count whether he wishes to or not. How many quiet unspectacular men do you and I know about whom their friends and neighbors say, "He is so hardheaded you cannot fool him; he looks on both sides of a question before he makes up his mind; and he always tries to be fair"? The influence of that man may reach only a few people, and by itself it does not loom very large. But multiplied a million times over it has controlling importance, for it is the raw material out of which must be built the public opinion on which we must depend to preserve our civil liberties and guarantee the safety of American democracy.

CIVIL RIGHTS AND THE FEDERAL LAW

BY FRANCIS BIDDLE

Attorney General of the United States

THE THEME of this paper is not the definition of "civil rights" or the discussion of the philosophy underlying them or of the history of the struggle of men to achieve their civil liberties, but rather the story of their crystallization in federal law, especially in the guarantees of the Federal Constitution and statutes.

To understand the temper and approach of the colonists as they declared their independence, fought for it, and then said what was to be in their new government, we must examine the Declaration of Independence and the Articles of Confederation. We think of the Declaration, rightly enough, as a charter of freedom. But it is also a passionate indictment by the men of the thirteen states, now united in a common cause, of the evils they had suffered at the hands of their sovereign. These were Englishmen telling another Englishman across the seas that he had acted like a tyrant and treated them like slaves. Men had a right to be free, they declared, to abolish their government when it became destructive, and to institute a new government. Prudence should be exercised before such action. Yet there was a point when men should no longer suffer. "But when a long train of abuses and usurpations, pursuing invariably the same Object evinces a design to reduce them under absolute Despotism, it is their right, it is their duty, to throw off such Government and to provide new Guards for their future security."

These were bitter men who would no longer be patient, and their bitterness was expressed in specific complaints against the King. "Let facts," they said, "be submitted to a candid world." The enumeration of their grievances comprises what might be called a great Bill of Wrongs.

It is important for our purposes, I think, to remember the temper in which the Declaration was framed, a temper of angry and bitter resentment of men who had known for generations a system of their own laws and a parliamentary government under those laws, and fiercely hated what they regarded as the present tyranny of the Crown.

This resentment and fear of government is reflected in the Articles of Confederation adopted five years after the Declaration, in 1781. The distrust of sovereignty was so great that there could be nothing more than "a firm league of friendship." Today the Articles read not unlike a hesitant League of Nations. The votes of nine states were needed to make war, coin, borrow, or appropriate money, and admit other states. But civil liberties did not have to be included, as they were obviously considered a matter for the states to deal with.

The "Ordinance for the government of the territory of the United States northwest of the river Ohio" was adopted by the Confederate Congress on July 13, 1787, six years after the signature of the Articles of Confederation. It expressed a compact between the states and the people, the first two articles of which protected civil liberties, providing that no person should "ever be molested on account of his mode of worship"; that the inhabitants should be entitled to the benefit of *habeas corpus* and trial by jury; that all persons should be bailable unless for capital offenses; that no cruel or unusual punishment should be inflicted; that property should not be taken except for full compensation. Article III directed that, "The utmost good faith shall always be observed towards the Indians." Article VI outlawed slavery and involuntary servitude.

The delegates to the Constitutional Convention assembled in Philadelphia in the very year that the Northwest Ordinance was adopted. They followed closely John Dickinson's advice: "Experience must be our only guide, reason may mislead us." They avoided abstract statements as to the rights of man and soberly limited constitutional protection of individual rights to those for which Englishmen had fought throughout English history. Provision was made that the writ of *habeas corpus* should not be suspended, that there should be no bills of attainder or *ex post facto* laws. Trial by jury was guaranteed. Constructive treason, which might be considered the English equivalent of *lèse-majesté*, was abolished. Religious tests for public office were prohibited. But no provision was made for the protection of the great personal rights of freedom of speech, of religion, of the press, and of assembly.

Bills of rights giving positive protection to these freedoms and guaranteeing the security of person and property, and even the right of revolution, had already been adopted in many of the states. When the Constitution was submitted to the states for ratification, at once a great popular demand arose that there should be similar guarantees against governmental interference with these rights in the Federal Constitution. Massachusetts even drafted proposed amendments which she later submitted to the national government before she ratified the Constitution.

In the First Congress in 1789, the first ten amendments, our present Federal Bill of Rights, were passed by Congress and submitted to the people practically as a part of the original Constitution.

These amendments forbade Congress to make any law interfering with the freedom of religion, of speech, or of the press, or with the right of assembly and petition. They gave protection against unreasonable searches and seizures, provided for due process, and prohibited the taking of private property without compensation—all fundamental safeguards of the individual against abuses by his national government. These guarantees were for the most part negative, directed against the federal government only, and giving that government no power to protect fundamental personal rights by legislation against infringement either by the states or by individuals. It was the violation of liberties by government that the citizens of those days feared, and especially the power of a great federal government which might meddle unduly with the affairs of their states, with which the citizens felt a closer tie.

From the foundation of our government until 1865, the citizen looked not to the nation but to his state as the source of his rights and liberties, and for his protection.

Immediately following the Civil War new problems made necessary a new approach to the question of protection of individual rights. The defeat of the South carried with it for a time a weakening of the old doctrine of states' rights. The national government rather than the states became at that time the proponent of liberal doctrine. The immediate problem of the nation was the establishment of genuine freedom for the Negro, who had been released only from chattel slavery by the Emancipation Proclamation.

The first step in the program was the adoption in 1865 of the Thirteenth Amendment, which abolished both slavery and involuntary servitude throughout the nation and gave Congress the power to make its provisions effective by appropriate legislation. As the Supreme Court has said in the present term, this amendment guaranteed that there should not only be an end to slavery, but that a system of completely free and voluntary labor should be maintained throughout the United States. It was soon clear that such a guarantee would not be self-enforcing.

In the *Dred Scott* [1] case, Chief Justice Taney had

---

[1] *Dred Scott* v. *Sandford,* 60 U.S. 393 (1856).

declared that a free Negro had no standing in the federal courts since he was not a citizen of the United States and could not become one by virtue of his citizenship in any one state. At the time of the adoption of the Constitution, the Justice contended, all Negroes were "articles of merchandise," not part of the sovereign people or inheritors of the "blessings of liberty" and "had no rights which the white man was bound to respect." Freedmen, having "been subjugated by the dominant race . . . remained subject to their authority and had no rights or privileges but such as those who held the power and the Government might choose to grant them."

Acting on these principles, the Southern states immediately after the War proceeded to pass legislation, known as "Black Codes," directed specifically at the freedmen with the purpose of organizing them into subservient agricultural laborers. Special labor, apprentice, and vagrancy statutes were enacted which resulted in penalizing any Negro who was not continuously industrious, preferably working for a white employer. In some cases the Negroes were forbidden to cross county or parish lines without a permit and were required to be able to show that they were working for a white employer.

The first Civil Rights Act of 1866 was passed, under the authority of the Thirteenth Amendment, to do away with these practices. In the same Congress the Freedmen's Bureau was established. The power of Congress to pass the act was sharply challenged, and two months later the Fourteenth Amendment was submitted to the states.

The first section of this amendment provided: "All persons born or naturalized in the United States and subject to the jurisdiction thereof, are citizens of the United States and of the States wherein they reside. No State shall make or enforce any law which shall abridge the privileges or immunities of citizens of the United States; nor shall any State deprive any person of life, liberty, or property without due process of law." The Southern states refused to ratify the amendment, and as a result Congressional Reconstruction was instituted. The first Reconstruction Act was passed on March 2, 1867. Three others followed in rapid succession. The whole South was put under the control of military commanders. The whites were disfranchised and the Negroes enfranchised; new elections were held by a handpicked electorate under the supervision of the Army; constitutional conventions composed of "scalawags" and "carpetbaggers" framed new constitutions which put all political power in the hands of the group who would support the more radical Northern policies; and finally the Fourteenth Amendment was ratified. Seven reconstructed states were then readmitted to the Union under strenuous suffrage regulations.

Resistance by the white Southerners took the form of an underground revolutionary movement. The Ku Klux Klan, which was organized in 1866, originally as a social club of young men who could find no occupations in the postwar South, was disbanded in 1869. But the

Klan movement continued until Reconstruction ended in 1876. Resistance to the exercise of suffrage by the freedmen was particularly strong. To help meet this resistance, the Fifteenth Amendment, which forbids the denial of the right to vote on grounds of race or previous condition of servitude, was adopted in 1870. Shortly thereafter Congress passed the Civil Rights Act of 1870, popularly known as the Force Act, which reenacted the first Civil Rights Act of 1866, but was particularly intended to protect the right to vote.

Under the authority of this act and of the Reconstruction Act the troops policed the polls at election time, a practice which appears to have been continued in some places long after the formal end of Reconstruction. In 1880 we find a rider to an Army appropriation act to the effect that none of the money appropriated should "be paid for the subsistence, equipment, transportation, or compensation of any portion of the Army of the United States to be used as a police force to keep the peace at the polls at any election held within any State." [2] Apparently this direction was ignored by the Army so far as the troops in Beaufort County, South Carolina, were concerned. Local officials there report that the troops patrolled the polls until 1909, when they were specifically forbidden to do so any longer, and that until that time Negroes held local office in the county.

Southern resistance continued to be effective, and on March 23, 1871, President Grant sent a message to Congress in which he stated, "A condition of affairs now

---

[2] Walter L. Fleming, *Documentary History of Reconstruction* (Cleveland, 1907), II, 431.

exists in some of the States . . . rendering life and property insecure, and the carrying of the mails and the collection of the revenue dangerous." He added that the power to correct these evils was beyond the control of the state authorities and recommended legislation to secure the enforcement of law in all parts of the United States. In response a Joint Congressional Committee of Inquiry into the conditions in the Southern states reported the Klan to be the most dangerous element involved,[3] and the Act of April 20, 1871, was passed. In substance this act amounted to a federal anti-lynching statute.

Another drastic statute, the Anti-peonage Act, had been adopted under the authority of the Thirteenth Amendment, on March 2, 1867. It resulted from practices found to prevail in the Territory of New Mexico and inherited from the days of Spanish rule, but went beyond the particular evil involved and prohibited the holding of anyone in involuntary servitude anywhere in the United States. This is still a living law, used to eliminate the various indirect methods by which many persons of low economic status in many of the states have been forced to labor for a particular employer against their will. Recently the Supreme Court said that by this statute "Congress thus raised both a shield and a sword against forced labor because of debt."

Finally, in March, 1875, the last Civil Rights Act extended the prohibition against racial discrimination to service in inns, public conveyances, and places of public recreation.

---

[3] *Senate Reports*, 42 Cong., 2 Sess., No. 41, Pt. 1.

The changes brought about by such legislation were drastic, for they not only provided for federal control over acts that had heretofore been in the exclusive jurisdiction of the states, but affected underlying social relations. The balance of state and federal power was materially altered.

Taken together, the three amendments and the five statutes, all adopted over a period of eleven years for the express purpose of freeing the slaves, making them citizens, and giving them the right to vote, constitute an important chapter in the history of the theory and practice of equality before the law, an equality essential for the achievement of freedom. Today they constitute the sole source of the power of the federal government to protect individual rights against encroachment by the states and, in some instances, by individuals.

I propose to examine the Civil Rights Acts in some detail. The Act of 1866 undertook to overrule the *Dred Scott* decision by declaring, as does the Fourteenth Amendment, that all persons born in the United States thereby acquire a national citizenship. It provided that all citizens of the United States should be equally entitled to certain rights including the right "to make and enforce contracts, to sue, be parties, and give evidence, to inherit, purchase, lease, sell, hold, and convey real and personal property, and to full and equal benefit of all laws and proceedings for the security of persons and property"; and the right to "be subject to like punishment, pains, and penalties, and to none other, any law, statute, ordinance, regulation, or custom, to the contrary notwithstanding."

It was the theory of the proponents of the act that Congress had the power to pass it under the authority of the Thirteenth Amendment, and it was an attempt to set aside the state laws which were gradually imposing on the Negroes the very restrictions which had existed at the time of slavery. As Senator Stewart said, "It strikes at the renewal of any attempt to make those whom we have attempted to make free slaves or peons. That is the whole scope of the law." [4] Jurisdiction of all offenses under the act was placed in the federal courts, an extreme extension of federal jurisdiction. There were added special facilities for enforcement; the President was empowered to establish tribunals to prevent or punish offenses, and to use the land or naval forces "to prevent violation and enforce the due execution of this Act." The act provided for a direct appeal to the Supreme Court of the United States on all questions of law.

The constitutionality of the bill was violently challenged in Congress, but in spite of opposition it passed by a large majority in both Houses. It was then vetoed in a long message by Andrew Johnson.[5] Eleven out of thirty-six states, he pointed out, were not represented in the Congress. Were the newly enfranchised slaves prepared to exercise the responsibilities of citizenship? Congress, said the President, had no power to deal with

---

[4] *Cong. Globe*, LXX, 1785.
[5] *Cong. Globe*, LXX, II, 1679.

citizenship, a state prerogative. The act would create federal supervision over the administration of the law by local judges and other officials, and might penalize them even when they acted in accordance with the state statutes. Congress replied that that was indeed the very purpose of the act, and promptly passed it over the President's veto.

There seems little doubt that the Fourteenth Amendment was introduced two months later partly to solve the constitutional questions raised by the act of 1866, and that Justice Field was historically correct when he said in his dissent in the *Slaughterhouse Cases* that the rights, privileges, and immunities of citizens of the United States referred to in the first section of the Fourteenth Amendment included the rights enumerated in the first section of the act.

On May 31, 1870, after the adoption of the Fifteenth Amendment, the second civil rights statute was enacted.

The guarantees of the act of 1870 and the amending act of February 28, 1871, were very far-reaching. Penalties were included for any interference with an inhabitant in his right to qualify as a voter; interference with registration or with the exercise of the right of suffrage was made a crime; and there was introduced for the first time a conspiracy section. This related to conspiracies to injure, oppress, threaten, or intimidate any citizen with intent to prevent or hinder his free exercise and enjoyment of any right or privilege granted or secured to him by the Constitution or laws of the United States. The conspiracy was made a felony punishable by fine not to exceed five thousand dollars and by imprisonment up to ten years, and carried disability from thereafter holding any office of trust with the government. The penalties were extremely severe as applied to certain cases. The section, unaltered in substance, is now the famous Section 51, Title 18, of the United States Code, and forms the basis of a large number of the criminal actions brought by the Department of Justice to punish the violation of civil liberties.

The amendment of 1871 further provided that if in the act of depriving a citizen of federal rights or privileges, any other felony, crime, or misdemeanor should be committed, the offender should be subject to the same penalty in the federal courts for such crimes as he would under state law.

In addition, the act specifically penalized election frauds in connection with the election of a federal official. Election officials were to be punished for their failure to enforce state laws as well as federal laws; and any person who believed that he had lost an election because citizens had been denied the right to vote on account of race or color was given the right to bring suit to recover possession of the office in either the federal or the state courts.

The Act of April 20, 1871, "to enforce the provisions of the Fourteenth Amendment to the Constitution . . ." was the reply of Congress to the activities of the Ku Klux Klan and other lawless groups referred to in President Grant's message of March 23. It provided civil as well as criminal remedies for the deprivation of rights under color of law. Its provisions, spelled out in great detail, covered a broad field, and included a clause that if the state authorities were unable or unwilling to prevent the deprivation of a constitutional right, and violence resulted, the President was empowered to take appropriate measures to suppress the violence. Senator Frelinghuysen of New Jersey, in support of the section, said in Congress: [6]

A State denies equal protection whenever it fails to give it. Denying includes inaction as well as action. A state denies protection as effectually by not executing as by not making laws. . . . It is a poor comfort to a community that have been outraged by atrocities, for the officials to tell them, "We have excellent laws on our statute-books." It is the citizen's right to have laws for his protection, to have them executed, and it is the constitutional right and duty of the General Government to see to it that the fundamental rights of citizens of the United States are protected.

The person whose civil rights were injured was given a civil cause of action against the officer who should have protected him and did not, up to the sum of five thousand dollars. This was specifically directed against lynching and other forms of mob violence.

Finally, on March 1, 1875, an act was passed "to protect all citizens in their civil and legal rights." The preamble to this act reads as follows:

Whereas, it is essential to just government we recognize the equality of all men before the law, and hold that it is the duty of government in its dealings with the people to mete out equal and exact justice to all, of whatever nativity, race, color, or persuasion, religious or political; and it being the appropriate ob-

---

[6] *Cong. Globe*, XCVIII, 501.

ject of legislation to enact great fundamental principles into law . . .

Section 1 of the act required all inns, public conveyances, theaters, and other places of public amusement to open their accommodations to all persons regardless of race, color, or previous condition of servitude; and Section 2 made a violation of this provision a misdemeanor and gave the injured party a right to civil damages. All cases under the act were to be reviewable by the Supreme Court regardless of the sum of money involved.

The pendulum, following the carpetbag days and the rise of the Klan, had swung very far in one direction, carrying this great expanse of federal legislation, implemented by minute instructions for federal administrative machinery.

In the first test case in the Supreme Court of the United States, four years after the ratification of the Fourteenth Amendment, the swing began in the other direction. Faced with the prospect of the drastic extension of federal power implicit in the three constitutional amendments and the civil rights acts, the Supreme Court sided with Andrew Johnson rather than with Congress.

The *Slaughterhouse Cases* [7] did not involve any of the civil rights statutes, but a construction—the first— of the Fourteenth Amendment, which in effect greatly impaired the broad application of the amendment to those statutes. The state of Louisiana created by statute

[7] 83 U.S. 36 (1872).

a monopoly in a single corporation for slaughtering ani-
mals over a very wide territory. The Court, dividing five
to four, sustained the constitutionality of the grant,
which removed from all others the right to engage in
this business, on the ground that it was within the appropriate exercise of the state's police power to protect
the health of the community. With that decision we
are not concerned. But the argument was vigorously
pressed that the Fourteenth Amendment had made the
citizens of Louisiana also citizens of the United States
and had provided that no state could abridge their
privileges and immunities—here the privilege to engage in this lawful business. The majority opinion, delivered by Justice Miller, pointed out that there were
two kinds of citizenship—state and federal—and construed the Fourteenth Amendment to protect only
those rights springing from federal citizenship. The
rights claimed here sprang from state citizenship and
were therefore not "privileges and immunities of citizens of the United States," protected by the amendment. The majority could not conceive that the purpose
of the amendment was to "bring within the power of
Congress the entire domain of civil rights heretofore
belonging exclusively to the States."

Field, dissenting, said that was the very purpose of
the amendment. Calhoun had preached the doctrine
that there was no such thing as citizenship independent
of the citizenship of the state. The *Dred Scott* case had
held that citizenship in the United States was dependent upon citizenship in the several states. But the
amendment had settled the old dispute, had swept it

aside, making all persons born in the United States citizens and placing the common rights of American citizens under the protection of the national government. "The privileges and immunities designated are those which of right belong to the citizens of all free governments."

There were two other vigorous dissents. Bradley thought "it was the intention of the people of this country in adopting [the] amendment to provide National security against violation by the States of the fundamental rights of the citizen." Swayne pointed out that the three amendments were new departures, marking a new "epoch in the constitutional history of the country" by trenching directly on the power of the states. "Fairly construed," he added, "these amendments may be said to rise to the dignity of a new Magna Charta."

The effect of the decision was to remove from the purview of the criminal sections of the statutes the rights which are enumerated in the first section of the Act of 1866.

The pendulum was swinging and the impulse behind the great amendments was being cooled by the breath of judicial construction.

In 1882 the Court decided that the section which was intended to prevent lynching, was unconstitutional because it penalized individual action,[8] and the next year, in the *Civil Rights Cases*,[9] held unconstitutional the first two sections of the act of 1875. Five test cases were in-

---

[8] *U.S. v. Harris,* 106 U.S. 629 (1882).

[9] 109 U.S. 3 (1883).

volved. Stanley and Nichols had been denied accommodations at an inn; Ryan and Singleton at a theater; and criminal actions followed. Robinson sued the Memphis and Charleston Railroad Company to recover the penalty for refusing to allow his wife to ride in the ladies' car on account of her African descent. The Court, speaking through Justice Bradley, held the sections unconstitutional because it construed the Fourteenth Amendment to prohibit state not individual action, and to give the federal government no power to pass protective legislation. A contrary interpretation "would be to make Congress take the place of State legislatures and to supersede them. . . . Civil rights, such as are guaranteed by the Constitution against State aggression, cannot be impaired by the wrongful acts of individuals unsupported by State authority. . . ." In a word, innkeepers, railroads, and theaters could admit whites and exclude Negroes so long as the states had not by statute approved the discrimination!

Harlan, vigorously dissenting, felt the distinction to be tenuous and metaphysical: "I cannot resist the conclusion that the substance and spirit of the recent amendments of the Constitution have been sacrificed by a subtle and ingenious verbal criticism." The purpose of the first section was to prevent race discrimination. He cited Section 5 of the Fourteenth Amendment, that "Congress shall have the power to enforce, by appropriate legislation, the provisions of this article." Could any legislation be more appropriate? Under Article IV, Section 2, of the Constitution, providing that an escaping slave could not be discharged by reason of any law existing in the state to which he had escaped but should be delivered up, the Congress had passed the fugitive slave law of 1793 and the far more drastic law of 1850, which "placed at the disposal of the master seeking to recover his fugitive slave, substantially the whole power of the nation." The dissenting Justice asks eloquently: "Was it the purpose of the nation simply to destroy the institution, and then remit the race, theretofore held in bondage, to the several States for such protection, in their civil rights, . . . as those States, in their discretion, might choose to provide?" And finally: "I insist that the national legislature may, without transcending the limits of the Constitution, do for human liberty and the fundamental rights of American citizenship, what it did, with the sanction of this Court, for the protection of slavery and the rights of the masters of fugitive slaves."

Following the narrow path to which the *Slaughterhouse Cases* and the *Civil Rights Cases* pointed, the federal courts continued to limit the scope of the civil rights statutes. The meaning of the privileges and immunities clause was whittled away until the present Chief Justice could refer to it as the "almost forgotten" clause of the Fourteenth Amendment.[10] Similarly, while the due process clause was being extended by the courts to cases involving the protection of property, it was limited in its application to personal rights by decisions that the terms "liberty" and "property" did not include certain fundamental rights, such as the right to

---

[10] *Colgate* v. *Harvey*, 296 U.S. 404 (1935).

vote in state elections [11] or the right to run for state offices.[12] The Court decided that the conspiracy section of the Civil Rights Act could not constitutionally be invoked to protect citizens from interference by individuals with the right of peaceful assembly,[13] the right to be protected from lynching by individuals (i. e., not "officials"),[14] the right to organize for purposes of collective bargaining,[15] or the right to remain within a state.[16] The Court held unconstitutional the sections of the act of 1870 which protected the right to vote in state as well as in federal elections on the ground that their scope was not limited to discrimination on account of race.[17] As late as 1903 the government, accepting the early theory of Congress that the Thirteenth Amendment not only abolished chattel slavery but entitled all freedmen to equal rights, successfully prosecuted "Whitecappers" who had driven Negro sharecroppers from the rich delta land of Arkansas.[18] Three years later, however, the Supreme Court refused to apply this doctrine against the same "Whitecappers" who had driven Negroes away from their jobs on a railroad.[19] One more of the principles underlying the civil rights acts was nullified.

In short, the application of the criminal sanctions to

---

[11] *Green* v. *Mills,* 69 Fed. Rep. 852 (1895).

[12] *Taylor and Marshall* v. *Beckham* (1) 178 U.S. 548 (1900).

[13] *U.S.* v. *Cruikshank,* 92 U.S. 542 (1875).

[14] *U.S.* v. *Powell,* 212 U.S. 564 (1909).

[15] *U.S.* v. *Moore,* 129 Fed. Rep. 630 (1904).

[16] *U.S.* v. *Wheeler,* 254 U.S. 281 (1920).

[17] *U.S.* v. *Reese,* 92 U.S. 214 (1875).

[18] *U.S.* v. *Morris,* 125 Fed. Rep. 322 (1903).

[19] *Hodges* v. *U.S.,* 203 U.S. 1 (1906).

the protection of civil rights has come to be restricted mainly to cases in which state officials participate, or misuse their power, or to situations involving rights granted directly to individuals and guaranteed against individual infringement by the Federal Constitution or laws. For many years such rights were few in number, limited for the most part to those granted by the Thirteenth Amendment, and to rights under such laws as the homestead acts and other federal land laws.

Even before the congressional program was completed by the act of 1875, a Congressional weakening of the civil rights statutes had begun which paralleled that by the courts. The rearrangement which the acts underwent in the *Revised Statutes* of 1873 effectively concealed the whole scheme for the protection of rights established by the three amendments and five acts by separating their provisions under unrelated chapters of the *Revised Statutes*. The act of 1894 and the codification of 1909 repealed most of the sections protecting the franchise.

As a result we now have on the statute books only fragments of the original laws, arranged under four titles of the United States Code. Under Title 8, "Aliens and Nationality," are gathered parts of the original statutes. A chapter entitled "Elective Franchise" contains the section which declares it to be the right of all citizens to vote at any election from federal to school district without discrimination on account of race, the basis of the recent decision of *Smith* v. *Allwright*,[20] which declared that Negroes had the right to vote in

---

[20] 321 U.S. 649 (1944).

a Texas primary. The right to recover damages for wrongs resulting in deprivation of civil rights is preserved and still runs against any person who has knowledge of a conspiracy and fails to aid in preventing it; and there are on record cases in which this section has been used by the widows of victims of lynching to recover against officials who were responsible.

Sections of the statutes having to do with jurisdiction and procedure are found in the Judicial Code (Title 28), and under "War" (Title 50, § 203–204) lurk two sections empowering the President to employ the armed forces to suppress violence or conspiracy to deprive "any portion, or class of the people" of their constitutional rights. Under the Criminal Code (Title 18) appear five sections of which the first two (§51–52) deal respectively with conspiracy to injure persons in the exercise of civil rights and depriving persons of civil rights under color of state laws. It is under these two sections, and the peonage section, that substantially all the indictments concerned with criminal violations of civil rights are brought by the Department of Justice. For many years after the repealing act of 1894, these sections were little used and, like the privileges and immunities clause, were almost forgotten.

The present codification, therefore, remains as fragmentary and confusing as were the earlier codes.

In the second quarter of this century the field of the rights of individuals protected by federal law has been considerably broadened by legislation, and the Supreme Court has generally not felt it necessary to yield to the temptation to substitute its views of federal-state relations for those of Congress when such statutes were before it for constitutional construction. Thus, under the National Labor Relations Act collective bargaining is a right secured in most instances by the federal government. The right to wages under the Fair Labor Standards Act, rights under the Agricultural Adjustment Administration Act and the Social Security Acts, rights to the use of housing projects constructed under the Lanham Act, the rights of returning soldiers to re-employment under the Selective Service Act, and, if implemented by appropriate legislation, the rights of minority groups (particularly Negroes) not to be discriminated against in employment—all these are rights now secured by federal laws directed against individual as well as against state interference.

With the broadening of the field of federal civil rights there has come a quickened sense of their importance. One response in this country to the challenge of the ideals of democracy made by the new ideologies of Fascism and Communism has been a deepened realization of the values of a government based on a belief in the dignity and integrity of human beings. The Supreme Court has reflected this attitude in the attention it has given in recent years to the application of the due process clause to the protection of the personal rights of individuals. The bar, too, has awakened to a consciousness of the importance of civil rights, and to the realization that such rights are not self-enforcing even in a democracy. The American Bar Association and the National Lawyers Guild have recently established civil rights committees and have participated in cases affecting those rights. Both associations now admit Negroes to their membership.

In February, 1939, a Civil Liberties Unit (now the Civil Rights Section) was established in the Criminal Division of the Department of Justice. Its directives were to be found principally in the conspiracy section, the color of law section, and the antipeonage law. Its task was to re-establish this federal law as an effective instrument for the protection of individuals' rights.

Even before the establishment of the Unit, the Department had begun to test the application of the civil rights statutes to newly created federal rights. A long bitter struggle between employers and miners in Harlan County, Kentucky, was finally ended when the United States District Court sustained an indictment of the offending employers and their accomplices for interference with the right of the miners to organize, a right guaranteed by the National Labor Relations Act (the case resulted in a mistrial so that the decision never got to the Supreme Court). Similarly, shortly after the organization of the Unit, the violent opposition of a southern textile operator to unionization was ended by indictment under the civil rights statutes. Since the decisions in those two cases protected employees' rights under the National Labor Relations Act, violations in which local officials have connived have several times been checked simply by a reminder from the United States Attorneys that there is a federally guaranteed right to organize, and that interference with it may constitute a federal crime.

Once the Unit was established and its existence known, many complaints began to pour in. It is interesting to note that the large number of complaints in the war years, with the possible exception of those concerning the mistreatment of Jehovah's Witnesses, has not been due to the impact upon personal liberties of either the exercise of federal war powers or the mob spirit which is so often a by-product of war. Rather they appear to reflect the general awakening of the nation to the importance of the protection of civil rights. Complaints come not only from the victims and from the groups organized for the specific purpose of protecting civil liberties, but from fellow townsmen and neighbors of the victims, and, in many instances, from local law enforcement officials who find themselves powerless to deal with the situations which they report. Though the federal rights created in recent statutes have provided the Section with some of its most interesting problems of law, a very small proportion of the complaints relate to their violation. The great body of complaints is concerned with exactly the problems with which Congress sought to deal when it first enacted the civil rights statutes; that is, the general protection of the right to vote and of the other civil rights of the Negro.

And the denial of these rights—often merely of the right to live in peace—touches tragic irony when committed in the midst of a war fought to defend them elsewhere. A few months ago a young Negro soldier sent this letter to the President, who forwarded it to the Justice Department for investigation:

I am a corporal in the U.S. Army. I have been in the Army for 17 months and in England for 11 months. I am a Negro with an American heart, and has been doing my duties as an American soldier. I consider myself as one of the best. I have never had a punishment. I have been awarded the "good conduct medal," "good driving medal" and sharp shooting with a 30–30 rifle and carbine, and a key man with a 50 calibre machine gun.

I was sent some papers from the states a few days ago. And I read where colored people in my home city, New Iberia, La., were being beaten up and chased out of town. Enclosed in them my sisters husband . . . who is a teacher in a local school and was the Chairman of a war bond drive and raised over $5000 from the colored people in that city. They are being beaten up because they succeeded in getting a welding school for the colored. So they could build the tanks and ships we need so badly.

They forced them to leave their homes, and also beat up the colored doctors and ran them out of town. The colored people that remains behind is without medical care and my family is there. God knows what will happen to them.

I thought we were fighting to make this world a better place to live in. But it seems as though we colored boys are fighting in vain, and that offers little encouragement to me. I am giving the U. S. A. all I got, and would even die, but I think my people should be protected. I am asking you, Sir, to do all in your power to bring those people to justice and punish the guilty ones.

The first case handled by the new Unit which was sufficiently important to reach the Supreme Court [21] involved interference with the right to vote and arose

---

[21] *United States* v. *Classic,* 313 U.S. 299 (1941).

from the turbulent election in Louisiana in which the Huey Long machine was defeated. Sections 51 and 52 of Title 18 were invoked to penalize the miscounting and destruction of ballots in the primaries. The Court held that the right to vote in federal elections and to have one's vote counted as cast extended to voting at primaries, which were an integral part of the election process, and that the civil rights statutes were appropriately used to penalize violations of that right even though the primary had been unknown when the statute was enacted. In a second test case, *United States* v. *Saylor*,[22] decided May 22, 1944, which was the result of wholesale ballot box stuffing in Harlan County, Kentucky, the Supreme Court decided that such practices amounted to interference with the right to have one's vote counted as cast, which is implicit in the right to vote, and were punishable under Section 52. By these two cases, the power of the federal government to punish election frauds, which appeared to be lost with the repeal of the Enforcement Act in 1894, has been restored. On April 3, 1944, a civil rights damage suit, *Smith* v. *Allwright*,[23] resulted in the vindication of the right of Negroes to vote in the primaries. The extent to which this decision can be made effective will depend largely on public opinion, on which convictions for the violation of civil rights ultimately rest.

Cases brought under the Thirteenth Amendment and the antipeonage statute on both the civil and criminal side since the establishment of the Unit have substan-

---

[22] *United States* v. *Saylor*, 322 U.S. 385 (1944).
[23] 321 U.S. 649 (1944).

tially strengthened the federal guaranty of freedom from involuntary servitude. In *Taylor* v. *Georgia* [24] and *Pollock* v. *Williams*,[25] decided April 10, 1944, the labor contract statutes of Georgia and Florida were respectively declared unconstitutional. The latter case has placed the right to freedom from involuntary servitude on so broad a base that the way has been opened to an attack on the "enticing labor" and "emigrant agent" statutes, and on some of the vagrancy statutes and "work or fight" orders, which experience has proved to be in reality indirect means of enforcing involuntary servitude, especially against Negro farm hands and laborers.

After an interval of many years a number of prosecutions have been instituted for violations of the peonage statutes. This year the drive of the Unit against peonage culminated in the first prosecution in many years against a large plantation owner. Albert Sydney Johnson, who farmed some ten thousand acres in the rich black belt of Arkansas, had consistently terrorized both the Negro and white laborers on his plantation, threatening to kill them if they left his place, and lent color to these threats by always carrying a gun, a revolver, and a pair of brass knuckles. White men as well as black so feared him that they would slip away from his farm at night, leaving behind their possessions, including their standing crops. Finally a deputy sheriff reported the case to the federal government, and local officials and neighboring landowners as well as victims

---

[24] 315 U.S. 25 (1942).
[25] 322 U.S. 4 (1944).

gave statements to the F.B.I. investigators which made it possible for the government to develop a watertight case against Johnson. An indictment was readily obtained from the federal grand jury. The news spread abroad, and the large news agencies sent reporters to cover the trial. Johnson tried to bluster his way out by intimidating and bribing witnesses, but the government's case was so strong that once it was in Johnson pleaded guilty; he was promptly sentenced to two and a half years and sent to jail. The conviction received favorable notice in many Southern papers, and there seems little doubt that this case, following a series of convictions of lesser fry, has been effective in breaking up at least the direct practice of peonage.

In one case the peonage statute was put to a novel use. The keeper of a small roadhouse in Georgia was convicted of peonage because he held in involuntary servitude the girls who came voluntarily to accept employment as waitresses, forcing them also to serve as prostitutes. This man had openly boasted that no one could penalize him for his activities since the local officials would not dare to prosecute him and he had been very careful never to cross a state line with a girl so that the Mann Act would not apply. He is now serving a ten-year sentence in a federal penitentiary.

Probably the most important work of the Section, however, both because of the number and the variety of violations and the legal questions involved, has been the revitalizing and clarifying of the meaning and application of Section 52, which forbids the deprivation of rights under color of law. Prosecutions under this section have been instituted against sheriffs, police officers, justices of the peace, and even judges who have misused the power of office to deprive individuals either of due process of law or of equal protection of the law. The section was first invoked for this purpose in the case of a policeman who tortured a young Negro boy in an attempt to force from him a confession of a theft of which he was later acquitted. A demurrer to the indictment was overruled.[26]

The Department has attempted to use the civil rights criminal statutes for a purpose for which they were no doubt originally intended, the punishment of lynching. In one case where the jailor was involved with the lynching mob, an indictment was obtained but the defendants were acquitted. In another, which involved a manhunt by a sheriff and his posse in Illinois, a demurrer to the indictment was overruled and the trial will be held soon. As most lynchings occur after the arrest of the victim, it may be possible, in spite of *United States* v. *Harris,* to punish both members of the mob and delinquent officials whenever there is any form of official connivance or participation.

Section 52 was invoked with the general conspiracy statute to indict a group composed of a sheriff, a jail "trusty," and a shyster lawyer, who worked together through the operation of a notorious "kangaroo court" to extort sums of money from prisoners in the county jail.[27] This long-forgotten power of the government to use the civil rights statutes to penalize delinquent local

---

[26] *United States* v. *Sutherland,* 37 Fed. Supp. 344 (1940).
[27] *Culp* v. *United States,* 131 Fed. Rep. (2d) 93 (1942).

officials seems to be fully re-established by a case involving abuse of members of the sect of Jehovah's Witnesses.[28] In this case representatives of the group called upon a deputy sheriff and the chief of police to ask for protection against threatened violence by the townspeople. They were ushered into the police office and, after the sheriff had removed his badge in an effort to disassociate himself from his office, were forced to swallow large quantities of castor oil while the police officer looked on, and were then tied together with a rope and paraded through the streets of the town. The Court held that the defendants had acted under color of a law even though the sheriff derived his powers from the common law and not from any statute, and that they were guilty of denial of equal protection of the laws by refusing to intervene to save the victims from violence in accordance with the ordinary duty of police officers, a decision which reaffirmed the "inaction" theory of denial of equal protection which had been advanced by Senator Frelinghuysen and made the basis of Section 3 of the Act of April 20, 1871.

As a result of this case it seemed that there could no longer be any doubt of the power and duty of the federal government to prosecute cases of police brutality, and a number of prosecutions were instituted in South Carolina, Mississippi, and Georgia, most of which involved brutality of jailors towards Negro prisoners for the purpose of obtaining confessions. Local public opinion has become aroused against this type of official cruelty as a result of the disclosures in these cases. Many

---

[28] *Catlette* v. *United States,* 132 Fed. Rep. (2d) 902 (1943).

complaints were submitted to the Department by local officials, and, in some cases, pleas of guilty were obtained.

Since the Supreme Court has held on a number of occasions that confessions unlawfully obtained by state or local officials violate the due process clause of the Federal Constitution so as to render the trial illegal, it would seem reasonably to follow that in such cases the civil rights statutes, based on such violation, would be applicable. But the growth of our law is not exclusively or perhaps chiefly logical, particularly where considerations of federal and state authority and jurisdiction are involved. The imponderables of balance and degree play a part. Justice Frankfurter, in his concurring opinion in the recently decided case of *Snowden* v. *Hughes*,[29] suggested a doubt, a limitation of degree, springing from the old problem of the United States and state relationship, which has so long plagued the courts. The plaintiff had charged the misuse of power by local officials exercised under election statutes of the state of Illinois. Justice Frankfurter, in concurring in the result, expressed the warning that the question as to whether or not there has been a denial of equal protection of the laws within the meaning of the Fourteenth Amendment "is not to be resolved by abstract considerations such as the fact that every official who purports to wield power conferred by a state is *pro tanto* the state. Otherwise every illegal discrimination by a policeman on the beat would be state action for purpose of suit in a federal court."

---

[29] 321 U.S. 1, 16 (1944).

The issue is for the first time before the United States Supreme Court as the result of an appeal [30] from a conviction of a sheriff, deputy sheriff, and town police officer, all of whom were convicted and sentenced for acts of horrible brutality against a Negro, committed under color of law. The Negro had complained to the grand jury that the sheriff had wrongfully taken away from him and kept his pearl-handled revolver. The sheriff, enraged, arrested the Negro under a warrant which charged him with the theft of a tire, handcuffed him, and when he had brought him to the jailyard, beat him so violently and for so long a time that the Negro died shortly after being dragged into his cell in the jail. Such violence in the course of arrest is specifically forbidden by the laws of the state in which the outrage occurred. In the setting of this shocking crime, the Supreme Court must decide the abstract and highly technical question of whether or not *misuse* by a state officer of powers granted him by state authority constitute "state action" within the meaning of the Fourteenth Amendment.

Like all programs operating in a new field, each step must be taken with caution and judgment. The success of the Department in obtaining convictions from local juries, after establishing the law by a series of appeals, is in my belief owing to the care which has been used in refusing to bring cases where the evidence was not convincing or the offense serious. Gradually throughout the country a respect for and fear of the certainty of federal justice to punish crimes of this nature is being

---

[30] *Screws* v. *United States*, No. 42, Oct. Term, 1944.

built up. Federal statutes should not be invoked where the states act vigorously and sincerely to indict and to try. In most of these cases, particularly in the one to which I have just referred, the defense is calculated to play on the prejudice of the local jury against federal interference with states' rights and "Yankee" meddling from Washington. It has been our policy, therefore, to have the local United States Attorney try such cases, or where it seems advisable, some leading lawyer in the locality to represent the government. Handled in that way and particularly with the support of the local newspapers, the community can be made to feel that it is *their* government invoking *their* law, to vindicate the good name of *their* city.

It is interesting that in many of these cases the local public opinion and the local newspapers are supporting the government's stand. In the last case referred to, the *Atlanta Journal* said, in commenting on the result: "Georgia must become a synonym for equal justice to all, colored or white, humble or mighty." The editorial concluded that the decision "lends a new and encouraging stand against mob violence and brutality in the South."

There can be no doubt that liberal sentiment is increasing in many of the Southern states. But the change is necessarily slow. And those who are constantly urging "vigorous" enforcement of the federal criminal statutes in these cases should remember that enforcement ultimately depends on the education of public opinion.

FREEDOM TO
LEARN

BY EDMUND EZRA DAY

President of Cornell University

IT IS CHARACTERISTIC of the confusion of our times that the spokesmen of democracy are attempting new definitions of our fundamental freedoms. Some of these declarations have proposed bold and somewhat dubious extensions of the freedoms for which the American colonies fought the Revolution. Others have been little more than new expressions of the liberties we have long cherished. The freedom of which I wish to speak to you today is in a sense only a corollary of two of the most important civil liberties written into the American Bill of Rights by the Founding Fathers. I refer to two of the liberties included at the outset of the first ten amendments to our Constitution: freedom of speech and of the press.

Just why have we placed in American democracy so much stress on these two liberties? Surely not because we deem it important that we should individually have the privilege of saying whatever is on our minds. A much more significant purpose lies behind the guarantees of free speech and freedom of the press. The basic considerations have to do with the obvious requirement of intelligence in the electorate. Only an enlightened electorate can hope to establish a forward-looking and soundly progressive regime. And no electorate can possibly be enlightened save as it has access to knowledge, whether that knowledge come by word of mouth or from the printed page.

It follows that the essential values residing in freedom of speech and of the press actually lie at the receiving rather than the sending end of the lines of communication. The freedom without which democracy cannot survive is the freedom to listen, to read, to observe, to reflect; in short, the freedom to learn.

For several years we have been seeing the frightful impact on civilization of the barbaric practices of the modern dictators. We can now see how obtuse we were in our failure to get the full import of some of their early exhibitions of fanaticism. As we look back, we can plainly discern that nothing could have more clearly foreboded the evil to come than the burning of the books. In this act the dictators served notice that it was not only the bodies of men that were to be enslaved, but their minds and spirits as well. The loyalty that was to be demanded of all was to be an unthinking loyalty. Discipline was to be absolute; an end in itself, not a means to an end. Moral values were to be obliterated. The new order required blind obedience of its followers and abject submission of its victims.

This terrible threat of the would-be conquerors of the world has now been successfully countered. Neither the body nor the mind and spirit of man is going to be subjugated by the brutal forces they have employed.

But that does not mean, of course, that mankind is now assured of freedom. Long periods of further arduous effort will be required to effect those conditions of freedom to which mankind has long aspired. Meanwhile, those in whose hands the torch of civilization is carried must endeavor to see clearly what steps forward most need to be taken next. This is true in every phase of the pursuit of freedom. It is especially true of those phases which bear directly upon the mind and spirit of mankind. It is in this connection that I wish to direct your attention for a while to this freedom that is so profoundly important: freedom to learn.

Historic battles for freedom of thought and inquiry have been fought over many fields. Some of the fields in which fighting in the past has been most bitter are now far behind the fighting front. The field of religion is an example. Time was when it was dangerous to think and speak independently about God and the Church. Heresy was a high offense and cruelly punished. While this still may be true for those who wish to remain within a particular sect or congregation, it is no longer true for civilized society as a whole. Generally speaking, we are now free to accept and propagate whatever religious faith we will.

The same sort of sweeping advance has been made over the field of the natural sciences. Indeed, we now take free scientific inquiry so much for granted that it is difficult to think that certain hypotheses and findings regarding the solar system and the origin of species were once held to be a denial of the word of God and hence wholly blasphemous. Happily, religion has long since abandoned its opposition to the physical and biological sciences.

It is in the domain of the social studies that heavy fighting with respect to freedom of speech and inquiry still goes on. Here it it still dangerous to express certain views, or to pursue certain lines of investigation. Of course the fighting is no longer done with the old weapons or with the same techniques. There is now no formal inquisition, no burning at the stake, no direct application of physical force. The fact remains that the fighting is still very real and is resulting in heavy losses.

In order that I may be quite concrete in what I have to say at this point, I refer to three recent undertakings of the University which have encountered some of the powerful attacking forces which we all need to understand. These three projects are (1) the program of intensive study of Contemporary Russian Civilization; (2) the series of public lectures on Civil Liberty; and (3) the newly created State School of Industrial and Labor Relations.

During the summer terms of 1943 and 1944, a comprehensive program of instruction was offered by the University on Contemporary Russian Civilization. Back of the entire program lay the idea that it is of the utmost importance that America come to see Russia more clearly and accurately—this with a view to breaking through the widely held assumption that the world is no longer big enough to accommodate in peace a great Russia and a great United States of America. In short, the program was an effort to implement a fundamental faith that knowledge is a better bet than ignorance, however deep-seated may be the elements of doubt and controversy.

The second project took the form of a series of five public lectures given at the University recently. The five speakers were chosen for one or the other of two reasons: either they were well-known scholars who had given convincing evidence of sustained and scholarly interest in the subject of civil liberties, or they were men related in a highly responsible way to the government's interpretation of civil liberties in these difficult years of wartime regulation and restriction. The basic intent of the whole series was to interpret the adaptations of our concepts of civil liberty in the light of the dislocations and complexities of modern urban industrialized society at war.

The third project involves an important, perhaps somewhat daring, extension of the University's work into another field marked by wide controversy. The idea of the New York State School of Industrial and Labor Relations did not originate with anyone directly connected with Cornell. It came from the Joint Legislative Committee on Industrial and Labor Conditions, created by concurrent resolution of the Senate and Assembly of the state. It is my considered opinion that the new school has immense possibilities. Concrete plans with respect to the structure and activities of the School are now being developed by a temporary board of trustees which will make formal report to the Governor and next state legislature. The School will doubtless assume instructional, informational, and research functions, and is expected to offer a diversified teaching program both through extension and on the campus. It is expected that men serving the interests of both management and labor will, through the operations of the School, come to understand better the reciprocal rights and obligations of both sides of the industrial partnership.

So much for the design and essential purpose of these three University enterprises. The point I have to make is that all three have been vigorously attacked. The Russian program has been charged with being an attempt to indoctrinate young Americans with Communistic ideals. Cornell, it has been said, has conducted a school for "Reds." The lecture series on civil liberty has been described as politically "loaded." It is asserted that conspicuous New Dealers were given a chance to publicize their views without challenge from the opposition. The New York State School of Industrial and Labor Relations is said to involve a capitulation to organized labor. Predictions are made that it will introduce elements of chronic discord on the University campus.

In some ways it is hard to take seriously charges such as these. What conceivable reasons would Cornell have for selling out to the Communists or the New Dealers or organized labor? On their very face the charges are not plausible. Moreover, anyone willing to examine the complete record, which has been at all times freely available, could readily find out that the accusations have been without basis of fact. However, the charges were seriously made, were widely circulated, and were probably accepted by a large number of persons at face value. That damage was thus done to the University has to be taken for granted.

Perhaps you will say: "Well, what of it? The projects were put through, were they not? Nobody stopped the University from doing these things. The Board of Trustees and the Faculty supported them. Where do the restrictions on free speech and inquiry come in? It looks as if the University had been quite free to do as it pleased."

There is force to this line of argument, of course. In a very real sense the University has been quite free to venture. Despite the pressure of attacks from the outside, the Board of Trustees and the Faculty showed unyielding courage in their defense of the University's right "to give instruction in any study." Nevertheless, these attacks take their toll. They are bound to generate fears of one sort or another, and these fears in turn are likely to result in restraints. While we have successfully weathered the storm here at Cornell, we have had ample evidence of the methods by which effective restrictions on freedom of speech and inquiry persist in educational institutions even in democratic countries such as ours. These restrictions stem largely from the fear of the consequences either to the individual or to the institution.

The consequences that are ordinarily most feared take a number of different forms. Most of these may be blanketed under the phrases "bad publicity" and "impaired public relations." It is feared that attitudes toward the individual or the institution will become less favorable in important quarters. Prestige may be lowered; public opinion may become hostile. The adverse reactions may reach into circles where financial support is involved. Appropriations may be cut, subventions withdrawn, potential donors alienated. The mere idea that these developments may occur serves to bring pressure to bear. Restrictions on free speech and inquiry may no longer take overt form; there may no longer be any direct exercise of police power to keep thought and speech and inquiry within bounds; but an excessive concern for public relations may have the same effect and may exert powerful restricting influences.

In some institutions the response to these fears of injury is a policy of avoidance. Care is exercised to see that no fighting issues are raised. The means that are employed to this end are usually well disguised—conservative methods in the recruitment of staff, systematic discrimination in the matter of promotions and increases of pay. These and other administrative practices will, over the years, make sure that few, if any, members of staff whose utterances might cause trouble get into positions of influence and responsibility. It may suffice if the administration does nothing more than let it be somewhat vaguely known that "unwise" expressions of opinion on the part of the faculty will be viewed with administrative disfavor. Open dismissals on the score of radicalism are, of course, avoided; restrictions on academic freedom must not be thought to play any part in institutional policy. Nevertheless, restrictions on free speech and inquiry may be widely operative in the field of the social studies if administration pursues a policy of avoidance.

Surely no such policy befits an institution of higher education in a free country like ours. A college or university that is worth its salt must adopt and pursue a policy of forthright responsibility with respect to the advancement and dissemination of knowledge. It is the clear duty of educational institutions to be centers of insight and understanding. Their business is not to propagandize for any party or interest, however strong or respectable it may be. The great cause which they must consistently serve is the disinterested pursuit of truth.

This is no easy assignment. In fact, in times such as ours—times which may become even more difficult in the years following the war—this task of the colleges and universities is one of great complexity and tremendous consequence. The world is in a state of general confusion. Feelings have been widely embittered. Counsels, even among the intelligent and well-informed, vary and conflict almost beyond belief. Emotions are highly charged and the obstacles to objective study and interpretation were never more formidable. These very facts make it all the more important that the educational institutions of this and other democratic countries be allowed without hindrance to carry on their essential work—the untrammeled promotion of knowledge and understanding.

Certain conditions which pervade intellectual endeavor in the field of the social studies make this work especially difficult. At the outset we have to admit that validation or proof in the social sciences is rarely, if ever, as authoritative or conclusive as it is among the natural sciences. Social problems do not get solved definitively through the contributions of the social scientists. The problems get adjusted in such a way as to give rise to new and different problems; problems which, it is hoped, will prove less troublesome than those they displace. Even the experts are usually in rather serious disagreement, and scientific progress itself is difficult to discern. Small wonder that under these circumstances the lay public is inclined to take over and lead the debate.

But this confusion of tongues is not the only condition that troubles the social science field. The second factor is the universal prevalence of bias of one sort or another. There is no such thing as complete objectivity in the analysis and interpretation of social phenomena. Individuals are so inevitably the product of the social matrix in which they are born, reared, and live out their careers that they cannot be expected to lift themselves entirely out of the complex of social forces they are called upon to interpret. Sustained efforts to identify and reduce bias can be and are made; they can never be entirely successful.

Admitting these two underlying conditions of inquiry in the area of the social studies, what demands can reasonably be made of those who lead our efforts to achieve greater social understanding? The answer lies in steadfast individual and institutional observance of certain principles which are essential components of the setting without which freedom of the intellect cannot be successfully sustained. Intellectual honesty is the first of these principles. Although it may not be possible to rid ourselves entirely of bias, it is possible to display intellectual integrity. We all can also observe the rules of fair play in the exchange of ideas. Clearly enough, there is such a thing as good sportsmanship in the business of developing ideas. Contrariwise, there is such a thing as underhanded play, one of the most common forms of which is name calling. The hard-pressed debater who cannot meet the argument is prone to defame the arguer. Political life is, of course, full of this sort of thing. Still another feature of the arrangements essential for arriving at dependable knowledge is readiness to accept a balancing of competing views and suspected biases. Insistence on competence among the inquirers is also in order. A responsible relationship to the matters under examination may be said to be still another requisite of any serious study. Most basic of all in setting up the conditions of sound intellectual endeavor in fields ridden by controversy is an unfailing love of truth. Given conditions of intellectual integrity, fair play, competence, a sense of responsibility, and a consistent devotion to truth seeking, there should be no bar to untrammeled inquiry, however controversial may be the subjects with respect to which knowledge is sought.

All this would seem to be so eminently sound as to leave no room for serious differences of opinion with respect to the role which a great university should play. Free societies are sorely in need of well-protected centers of expanding knowledge and understanding. These centers must not be perverted into instruments of propaganda, no matter how deserving the causes which need to be served. Safeguarded as institutions devoted to the disinterested pursuit of truth, and meeting the many obligations which accompany the extraordinary freedom which they enjoy as institutions of higher learning, the universities should find favor with all classes and conditions of men who seek to promote more rational and humane relationships for all mankind.

The prospects of freedom brighten over the generations, but at times—and ours is one in point—the skies are clouded and shadows deepen. Great crises call for reaffirmations of faith. Let us renew our trust in the saving grace of wider sympathy and greater understanding. Let us dispel our fear of ideas and come to a full realization that the only effective way to combat bad ideas is with good ideas. Let us know that human conflict is more likely to stem from ignorance than from knowledge; that human progress can be more surely made in the light than in darkness. Let us realize now, and throughout our lives, that it is only as we strive for truth that we can achieve enduring freedom.

...r Services

7 Day Loan

...his item on or before the due date stamped below (if
...issue option users may write in the date themselves)

Fines are payable for late return